WATERSIDE WALKS

IN SUFFOLK

written and walked
by
Angus Pinney

Line Drawings by Julie Hobbs

Published by Minimax Books

ACKNOWLEDGEMENTS AND THANKS

Firstly, and most importantly, I must thank Viv who has accompanied me on all of these walks and put up with being led astray on some of them. Thanks also to other good friends who have kept me company on various walks and, I hope, enjoyed them. Thanks to Neil Lister for his help regarding the Shotley Peninsula Project. My introduction to the history of the coast and sandlings was particularly helped by the books of Robert Simper and Russell Edwards who both obviously share my love for the area but must have a much deeper knowledge than I can ever hope to approach. Lastly, thanks are due to Julie who has cheerfully drawn whatever I asked her to, with tremendous skill

ISBN 0 906791 82 0

© Angus Pinney

Published by Minimax Books Ltd
Broadgate House, Church Street,
Deeping St James, Peterborough

Printed in England by Watkiss Studios Limited

WATERSIDE WALKS IN SUFFOLK

by

Angus Pinney

Reed Bunting

Line Drawings

by

Julie Hobbs

CONTENTS

CONTENTS continued ....

Shelluck.

INTRODUCTION

Suffolk is a wonderful place and the coastal strip is the best part of this beautiful county. Within these pages I have attempted to give you an opportunity to share some of the walks I know so well and, at the same time, to share some of the bits and pieces of knowledge about the area and its history that I have gleaned over the years. Personally, I am not much interested in knowing, for instance, that a certain church has a 14th Century chancel so have tended to concentrate on the more quirky or human aspects of history and how they have affected the region.

The walks range from 8km (5 miles) to 20km (12.5 miles) and all but one have an extensive shortcut or two to be taken if required. After you have walked them the way suggested, try them backwards. Well, you know what I mean - it is surprising how different they look from the other direction.

The short essays which accompany the walks are really just a taster to awaken the interest. Hopefully, you will then feel like exploring the subjects in more depth by reading some of the books from the bibliography at the end.

Lastly, I hope that when you have completed the walks, enjoyed the sights and sounds of the coast and estuaries and, perhaps, supped in some of the many pubs along the way, you will have had at least some of the fun I have had in compiling this book.

ANGUS PINNEY
Spring 1996

Shore line Stump.

Wonderfully shaped shoreline stumps like this
can be seen along the riverside on the Holbrook Walk (No 20),
between points 6 and 7.

KEY TO MAPS.

DECIDUOUS WOODLAND

CONIFEROUS WOODLAND

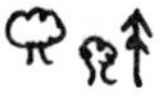

MIXED WOODLAND

WATER

BUILT UP AREA

PH   PUB

C   CAFE

T   TOILETS

CP   ALTERNATIVE CAR PARK

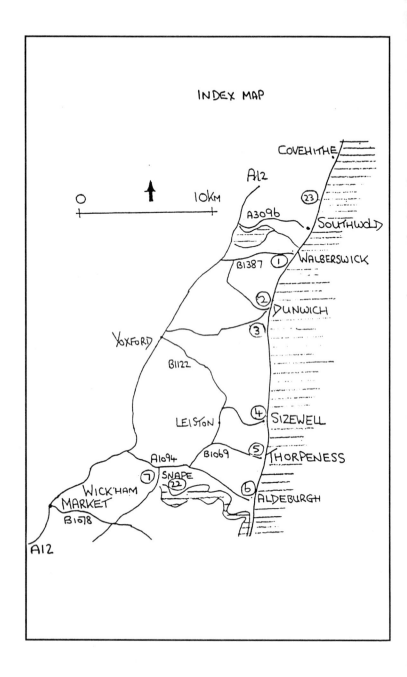

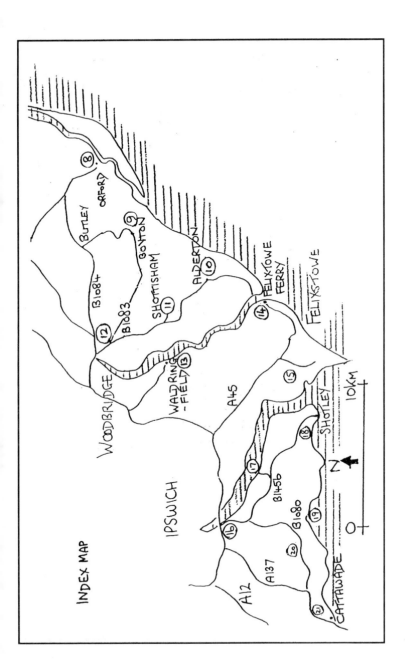

INDEX MAP

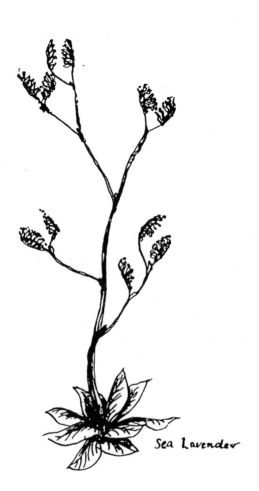

Sea Lavender

WALK ONE

Walberswick - Westwood Marshes - Newdelight Walks
- Walberswick Common - Walberswick

If only the Halesworth to Southwold Railway was in operation today, what a marvellous attraction it would be - especially if some of the old conditions of travel were in operation.

The track was opened in 1875 and, especially after it had passed Blythburgh, covered some of the finest scenery in Suffolk. There is a wonderful combination of woodland, river estuary, reed beds and wild open heath. The rolling stock for the 3ft guage line was constructed by Ransomes of Ipswich who had experience of building narrow guage rolling stock for export to China; some of the Chinese style of tramcar seems to have remained, with open ended verandahs and tramway style seats inside. Indeed it is said that the line used the coaches the Chinese no longer required and that the Chinese Imperial Dragon could just be discerned beneath the local maroon livery. Described as airy and spacious, straw was supplied on cold days to keep the passengers' feet warm. Straw coaches, with attendant goods wagons, were hauled by a tiny blue engine which sometimes found the going so difficult that a team of horses was required to help it up the Halesworth Incline.

The pace of life was obviously a lot slower a century or so ago: with a maximum speed of 16mph the little train took a leisurely trip across the heath and marshes. So much so that, on occasions, the driver would stop to set his rabbit snares on the journey one way and collect his catch on the way back!

A major engineering feature of the line was the swing bridge over the river as the track neared Southwold: it could be turned sideways to allow boats through. The bridge consisted of a bowstring girder which turned on a steel caisson sunk in the river bed but, unfortunately, it had to be destroyed during the Second World War as one of the many precautions against invasion along this part of the coast.

The Line flourished for almost 50 years and at its peak, around 1910, was carrying over 100,000 passengers a year and almost 15,000 tons of freight. The coming of buses to Southwold in 1928, with their amazingly fast speed of 20mph, and the decline of the Southwold herring fleet, meant that losses set in and the last passenger service ran on April 11th, 1929.

As an interesting footnote, one of the only two fatal accidents on the line occurred in 1883 when the 17-year-old in charge of Walberswick station boarded a moving train. Imagine a 17-year-old stationmaster today!

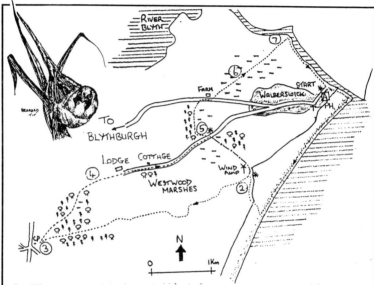

A. The car park is situated on the area known as Fisherman's Flats, which is where the fishermen used to lay their nets out to dry.

The Walk - 14.5km (9 miles)
Shorter Walk is 8.5km (5.25 miles)

This is a walk around Walberswick, its surrounding marshes and heaths. Park in the carpark at the end of the road in Walberswick. Refreshment is available at the Bell Inn and the craft rooms tea shop.

START: Make your way to the beach near the river mouth and turn right to walk along the shingle towards Dunwich. Just after you draw level with the derelict windpump on the marshes, look out for a path taking you inland.

2. Approximately 50 metres before you reach the windpump, take the path on your left. *** This path takes you through reed beds and woodland onto heathland.

3. As you approach the small car park at the crossroads, a track comes in from behind you on your right. Take this to head back towards Walberswick.

4. Walk along this track for 4km, going uphill past the large Westwood Lodge and later a small cottage on your left, until you come to open heath on your left. ***

5. Take the signposted path over the heath, following this all the way to the road. Turn right and just after the farm, left onto the heath.

6. At the crossway of paths, go through the gate and straight ahead on either of the two paths. When you reach the tarmac path, turn left to the river.

7. Turn right to walk down the river and back to the start.

*** SHORTCUT: as you reach the windpump continue straight ahead, passing just to the right of the pump. Go uphill through woods and heath to the road. Rejoin the main path by crossing onto the heath.

WALK TWO

Dunwich - Dunwich Forest - Westwood Marshes - Newdelight Walks - Hinton - Westleton - Dunwich Heath - Dunwich

In the 18th and 19th centuries navigation was not the exact science it has, with the help of satellites, become today. The Suffolk coast, with its myriad of shifting sand and shingle banks and bars, saw the wreck of many a good ship.

The beach companies situated all the way along the coast from Lowestoft down to Felixstowe Ferry were formed to cater for all the needs of passing shipping, providing services such as supplying food and other stores, putting pilots on board and, when wrecks occurred in these tricky waters, carrying out rescue and salvage operations.

Good lookout points were needed and the two towers situated on the front at Aldeburgh were originally built by the two competing beach companies in the town, the Uptowners and the Downtowners. One of the conventions of the beach companies was that whoever reached a wreck first was rewarded with salvage of that boat. If it was provisioning that was required, that too was provided by the first to reach the 'customer'.

The beach yawls used were, therefore, sleek double ended boats built for speed, between 40 and 70 feet long with large lugsails which needed very careful handling.

When the RNLI introduced 'proper' lifeboats along the coast from 1801 onwards they were not well received by the beachmen. By the end of the century they were replaced by the Norfolk and Suffolk lifeboat designed by the naval architect G L Watson in response to their complaints. The design was based on that of the beach yawl which sailed well and could be used in very shallow waters. The largest sailing lifeboat in England was operated in Aldeburgh from 1902 to 1928.

In time, with the development of the fishing industry which gave more regular employment and the increase in the number of steamships, allied to better organisation of the RNLI, the companies began to decline. The Felixstowe Ferry Beach Company was one of the last to keep a boat operating. Ablet Passiful, with his smacks

'Violet' and 'Wonder', organised the company and their yawl, 'The Pride of the Deben', was kept on the beach in front of the Martello tower. It was last used in 1915 to remove gear from a steamer aground on Shipwash Sands.

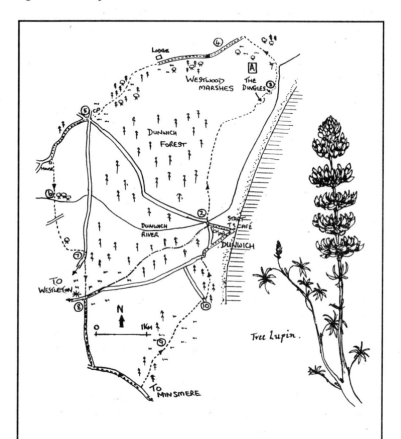

Tree Lupin.

A. Westwood Marshes are now one of the largest reedbeds in England. The water meadows were once drained by the now derelict windpump, and were flooded in the Second World War as a precaution against German invasion. Instead, reeds soon invaded to give the great habitat for marshland birds, such as marsh harriers and bitterns, that we have today.

The Walk - 20km (12.5 miles)
Shorter Walk is 16.5km (10.25 miles)

This is the longest walk of the collection and one of the best in the book. It has everything: woods, marshes, heathland, water, open fields and little used lanes. Start from the Dunwich beach carpark or, alternatively, the small car parking area at Newdelight Walks. Refreshment is available at the beach cafe or the Ship Inn at Dunwich.

START: From the carpark, walk to the village and go along the road past the Ship Inn. Walk past the church and, just after crossing a stream, take the track off to your right.

2. This track runs along the edge of Dunwich Forest as far as the Dingles (two small hills on Westwood Marshes). At the end of the track, pass to the right of the house and, after passing round the hillock, bear left to gain the raised causeway crossing to Little Dingle. Pass round this, again to the right, then follow the path to a T-junction.

3. Turn left and follow the path to the right of the ruined mill to the woodland and heath opposite. Go through this until you reach the road and turn left.

4. Follow the road until it turns into a broad sandy track and runs downhill, eventually emerging at a crossing of several roads.

5. Go straight ahead on the road signposted to Hinton. When you reach a postbox by the first houses on your left, go behind the sheds to a footpath along an old green lane. Due to the clutter on this track it may be necessary to walk on the adjacent field edge on your left. The path emerges into open fields. Continue ahead, keeping the hedge on your right.

6. Where the path enters woods, take the less well marked path straight on, crossing a stream and going up the hill opposite. Cross

the road and after crossing open fields and passing a wood and a pit on your left, bear left to the road.

7. Turn right and, after ignoring the main route into the woods on your left, take the oblique track a few yards further on through large gorse bushes. This brings you out opposite the road to Minsmere. ***

8. Take this generally quiet road towards the reserve. After just over 1km the road turns to the left. Follow the road round for a further 1km then take the well marked bridleway off to the left towards Dunwich Heath.

9. Ignoring paths to left and right, continue straight on with the path occasionally narrowing until you reach the road.

10. Turn right, then quickly left, into the woods. Follow the path to the road on the outskirts of Dunwich. Turn right to follow the road into the village. ***

*** SHORTCUT: At the road, turn left and at the corner take the track ahead. You are crossing the heath and woods in a nearly straight line. The only two places where you may be deflected from this course are, firstly, where the main track turns left to a gate and, later, in the woods where you have a choice of three paths. One marked blue goes to the right and one marked yellow goes at a right angle to the left. You continue straight ahead on the uncoloured path. At the church, take the road signposted to Dunwich Beach, turning left after you pass the Ship Inn.

Disused Windpump
on
Westward Marshes.

WALK THREE

Dunwich - Minsmere Sluice - Eastbridge - Middleton - Westleton Heath - Dunwich

Most of the butterflies still around in Suffolk today can be found in the coastal and rivers strip covered in this book. Regrettably, over the years Suffolk has lost more species than any other county and, of the 50 ever recorded, 21 have now disappeared. Several of these butterfly extinctions were many years ago but even since 1950 eight further species have had to be added to the list.

The walks in this book cover a variety of grass, woodland and, perhaps most important from a butterfly point of view, heathland habitats.

The history of the Suffolk heaths is a murky one indeed. The Sandlings Heaths covering much of the coastal strip have largely disappeared beneath a combination of afforestation, agriculture and, in more recent years, airfield construction and house building. The butterfly which has suffered most from all this is the Silver Studded Blue. In 1984, when Sainsbury's wanted to build a supermarket at Warren Heath, on the outskirts of Ipswich, a misguided attempt was made to physically transfer a section of heathland to an area nearby to maintain a population of this butterfly. Not enough was known of its close association with the black garden ant (the female lays its eggs in the ants nests) and, not surprisingly, the attempt failed and the population

Meadow Brown.

Ringlet.

Painted Lady.

Tortoiseshell

Small Heath.

22

was lost

The sandlings were kept in fine heathland condition by grazing with sheep and, later, by rabbits. With the introduction of myxamatosis in the 1950's and the consequent substantial decline of the rabbit population, there has been a great increase in gorse, bracken, silver birch and pine. Volunteers from conservation organisations such as the Suffolk Wildlife Trust spend many long and tedious hours playing at being rabbits, removing these intrusive species in an attempt to maintain some heathland habitat.

The coastal strip is where many of the grassland loving and migrant butterflies can be found, especially along the grassy river walls and watermeadows. I well remember a walk up the Orwell in the summer of 1992 when clouds of brown butterflies, with the more colourful Peacocks, Red Admirals and Painted Ladies, were flushed from the grass in front of me.

At the end of the war, Bentley Woods (Walk 21) were described as a fine a place as any in England for the number of species of butterfly to be seen and that is still so today. Even Tunstall Forest, with its large conifer plantations, has its good points: it provides the only place in Suffolk for the White Admiral and Dingy Skipper, as well as assisting with the return of the Speckled Wood. Heathland species such as Grayling, Small Heath and Brown Argus all like the wide fire breaks and open rides.

Dunwich Beach

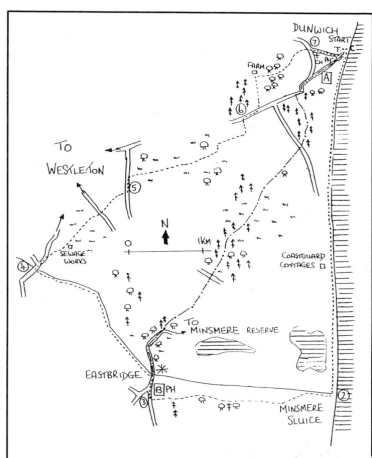

A. Dunwich is one of the few places to have a plant named after it. The Dunwich, or Burnet, Rose has leaves resembling salad burnet with creamy white flowers and purple-black hips.

B. The Eel's Foot Inn may have got its name as a corruption of 'Neale's boot'. John Neale was a mediaeval priest who thought he had managed to trap the devil in his boot. He hurled the boot into the Minsmere River to drown him but the devil managed to escape, having turned himself into a water serpent or eel.

The Walk (16km - 10 miles)
Shorter Walk is 11.5km (7.25 miles)

Park at the Dunwich beach car park or at Eastbridge. Refreshments in Dunwich at the beach cafe or the Ship Inn, or at the Eel's Foot Inn at Eastbridge.

START: From the beach car park, walk to the sea shore and head along the beach to your right. If you find walking on the shingle too tiring, there are steps up on to the heath after a while. If you stay down on the beach, wait until the cliffs end and find the path ahead running parallel to the beach and the Minsmere Bird Reserve.

2. At Minsmere Sluice, turn right to follow the left hand bank of the river as it heads inland. Where the track forks, go through the gate on your right and, later, follow the signs for Eastbridge.

3. Turn right on reaching the road and pass through Eastbridge. *** Just before reaching the river, turn left on the riverside path. It is best to keep to the raised riverbank rather than passing through the meadows, even if this seems more awkward at first glance, as barbed wire and boggy areas can be encountered at the far end.

4. Turn right over the bridge and, after 200m, take the oblique track off to your right. After passing the sewage farm on the right you come to a narrow road. Cross and continue to a second road.

5. Turn left and after 200m right, across a stile into an area covered in gorse and heather. Follow the well marked path across this heath-land for over 1.5km. On reaching a stile, turn left for a few metres then right to follow the right hand edge of the fields to a bungalow. Turn left on a track to the road.

6. At the road, turn right and, after passing forest and field on your left, turn left on the track opposite the entrance to Mount Pleasant Farm. When you reach the T-junction, turn right on the narrow path between high hedges.

7. On emerging at the road junction, take the road signposted to Dunwich Beach. Turn left after passing the Ship Inn, back to the car park. ***

***SHORTCUT: Continue along the road towards the Minsmere reserve. As the road turns right for the second time, take the signposted bridleway straight ahead, uphill. Cross the road and continue towards Dunwich Heath. Ignoring paths on either side, continue to the road. Turn right, then quickly left, to follow the path to the outskirts of Dunwich. At the road, turn right and follow it back to the start.

As you sit enjoying your drink in the Eel's Foot, reflect back to December 11th, 1747, when the area around the inn was the scene of a short engagement between dragoons working for the revenue men and a band of about 30 smugglers. The customs officers had previously learnt of a landing of goods at Sizewell Gap and, with the aid of Lt. Dunn of the Royal Welch Fusiliers, planned to capture the smugglers on the beach. Resistance was strong, however, and the soldiers were forced to retreat, surprisingly not to their base, but to the nearest inn. While they were enjoying their ale, the party of smugglers rode into the yard of the Eel's Foot. The dragoons went out to confront them and though, in the ensuing melee, most of the smugglers escaped, two were captured. Such was the strength of the smuggling gangs in Suffolk at this time, that the only safe way to transport these men for trial was by sea. So, under a guard of two sergeants and 12 privates, they were taken round the coast to London.

WALK FOUR

Sizewell - Dunwich - Dunwich Heath - Eastbridge - Sizewell

With its long and often deserted coastline and multitude of rivers and creeks, Suffolk has long been a haven for smuggling of all kinds. As soon as the government imposes a tax on any substance it is given a false price and offers immediate opportunities for anyone wishing to evade that tax.

Suffolk and its neighbouring counties became involved in smuggling as early as 1275 when a tax was imposed on wool exports, to protect English cloth makers from competition from foreign weavers who were able to undercut them using the same wool. The tax was so widely avoided that by 1662 it was felt necessary to punish illegal export by death! However, it was not until the centre of the weaving industry moved from East Anglia to the North, and new materials were introduced, that the tax fell and wool smuggling ceased. It is interesting to note that, to begin with, most smuggling was out of the country rather than into it. Customs officers in the late 1500's complained about the amount of corn and butter, as well as wool, that was being smuggled out of the country.

By the time wool smuggling ceased, local fishermen were looking for new ways to make money and the general expansion of wealth around that time meant that a trade in luxury goods developed. Britain was an expanding world power and had to raise revenue to develop and defend its interests. By 1760 around 800 imported items, ranging from coffin nails to snuff, were being taxed, presenting many an opening for enterprising smugglers. The most popular items were gin (or geneva as it was known, from the French for juniper, genievre, berries of which are used to flavour the spirit), rum, tea and tobacco. In 1733 the customs controller at Aldeburgh was Robert Crabbe, the grandfather of the poet, George Crabbe. He and his fellow officers seized 54,000 lbs of tea and 12,300 gallons of brandy along the coast from Kent to Suffolk that year, but it was estimated that only a very small part of the total amount being smuggled was intercepted!

"Brandy for the parson, Baccy for the clerk". So run the first lines of Rudyard Kipling's poem, which gives some idea of how much the local community supported the smugglers rather than the revenue men. Hiding places for contraband were varied and numerous, ranging from the obvious ones in local inns, to holes dug on Dunwich and Sizewell Heaths and disguised with broken branches and bracken. Farmhouses were favourites but perhaps the most unlikely places were the Quaker Meeting House in Leiston and under the pulpit of St Margaret's Rishangles.

Sometimes the smuggling operations were so large, with so many people involved in them, that the excise men could only stand and watch the goods being landed, without interference. In the second half of 1745, at the peak of the smuggling boom, it has been estimated that over 4,500 horse loads of contraband were landed in Suffolk. Much of that would have been landed at Sizewell Gap or Dunwich, the main centres of operations. The largest of these landings, at Sizewell, involved 300 horses and 100 carts on the beach at the same time!

After the end of the Napoleonic wars in 1815, many more men and resources were devoted to denying safe landing sites to the smugglers. This, and the use of the chain of Martello towers as watch towers, meant the enormous flow of contraband was slowed if not stopped. Even today, customs officers are busy all the time on this lonely coast in the constant fight against drug smuggling.

The Walk (15km - 9.75 miles)
Shorter Walk is 11km (6.75 miles)

I normally start this walk at Sizewell, though you could start either at Dunwich Heath or Eastbridge. Refreshments are available at the beach cafe in Sizewell, the National Trust tea shop at Dunwich Heath or the Eel's Foot Inn at Eastbridge.

START: Park at the beachside car part at Sizewell and go down to the beach. Turn left and follow the path in front of the power station. Carry on through the dunes and along the beach *** until you reach the coastguard cottages at Dunwich Heath.

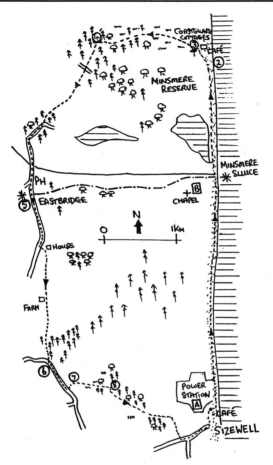

A. The St Paul's like dome on Sizewell B Power Station was lifted into place by the world's largest crane. Capable of lifting 1,200 tons, it took 71 lorries to bring it to Sizewell.

B. If you look very closely across to the ruined chapel, you can just make out the shape of a hidden pill box inside the walls. I wonder who would have been more surprised, the large invasion force storming ashore or the few defenders hidden in the chapel?

2. Take the track up the cliff and go to the left of the cottages where you will find a signpost directng you to Eastbridge. Go to the right of the toilet block to reach a broad track after about 100m.

3. Turn left to cross the heath. After 1km, as the track nears woodland and swings to the right, turn left from it, downhill, on a minor track.

4. You eventually will come to a T-junction with a broad track coming in from your right. Turn left and go straight ahead, following the track as it crosses a road then, when it joins another road, all the way to the village of Eastbridge. ***

5. Continue through the village and after almost 1km take the footpath on your left to an isolated house. Turn right and follow the bridleway until you reach the road.

6. Turn left and walk along the main road, (impossible to avoid, I'm afraid). 50m after passing the household waste tip, turn left and, after another 50m, right over a stile into a meadow.

7. Cross the meadow diagonally to your left, go over a stile and then continue to bear left to another stile on the edge of woodland. Follow the path through the woods to a track.

8. Turn right, then quickly left, and follow the track all the way to the road. Turn left to return to your starting point.

*** SHORTCUT: At Minsmere Sluice (just after the ruined chapel) turn left to follow the Minsmere river as it goes inland. Where the track forks, go through the gate on your right and, later, follow the signs for Eastbridge. Turn left at the road.

Turnstone

WALK FIVE

Thorpeness - Sizewell - North Warren - Thorpeness

The plants that grow along the coast have been put to all sorts of different uses, some of them quite interesting.

Sea holly, containing saponin, was used as far back as mediaeval times as a cure all. The roots were used to open obstructions of the spleen and liver, to cure jaundice, dropsy and the wind, as well as defects in the kidneys and lungs. It was even effective against the French Pox - whatever dreadful disease that was! As a bonus, sea holly was also an aphrodisiac but its best known use was for sweet making. Its Latin name is Eryngium and the sweets produced were known as Eringoes.

Robert Buxton, who was Mayor of Colchester in the middle of the 17th Century, seems to have been the first person to make Eringoes commercially. He took some of the roots, which surprisingly run to a depth of about 6ft, boiled them, then soaked them in cold water for several days. The pith was removed and the roots were then twisted into something resembling a barley sugar stick. They were then soaked in sugar solution and delicately flavoured with orange, cinnamon or rosewater. To preserve them, they were sometimes tinned.

Marhsmallows were, of course, made from the roots of the marshmallow plant. When boiled they give rise to a sort of slimy mucillage to which flavours could be added. Again, a plant well used in early medicine, Culpepper claimed that marshmallow boiled in wine cured coughs, hoarseness, shortage of breath and the swellings in womens' breasts. It was used as a poultice to reduce inflammation, swellings and any general pains. Teething babies could gain some respite by chewing the dried roots.

Sea pea and sea kale were other useful plants. The sea pea reputedly saved the people of Orford during a famine in the Middle Ages and sea kale, also known by its local name of Sickels, was used for its roots. Delicious fried in breadcrumbs and sprinkled with lemon juice, they were then served on toast with butter, or boiled and eaten like asparagus.

Lastly we come to the most widely used plant of all which is marsh samphire. Abundant on the saltings up and down the Suffolk rivers, it is considered a delicacy, and often eaten fried with bacon for breakfast. Sometimes it would be mown like hay, then gathered in large heaps and burnt over a hole in the ground into which the ash fell. This was soda ash, used in soap and glass making, from which the plant's alternative name of glasswort comes.

The Walk (14.5km - 9 miles)
Shorter Walk is 9.5km (6 miles)

A pleasant walk around Thorpeness, Sizewell and the North Warren RSPB Reserve. Park at the car park in Thorpeness and the best place for refreshment is The Gallery Coffee Shop nearby.

START: Make your way down to the seashore and turn left to go along the beach for 3km. If you find walking on the shingle too tiring, there is a footpath running along the cliff. When you reach the old coastguard lookout at Sizewell, turn inland to the road. After passing the pub, take the road on your left.

2. After about 300m turn right by a small thatched cottage down a track. On reaching a junction of several paths, turn left on a track. When you come to another broad track, turn right and, after passing a large house on the hill to your left, you come to a spot where the track forks.

3. Take the right hand fork and, as this track rejoins the main track, go immediately right again. After passing through the derelict railway bridge, turn right across the golf course. Just before you reach the green with cottages behind it to your left, turn left to pass in front of the cottages then take the track ahead. Follow this track to the road.

4. Cross the road and at the T-junction of paths turn right. This brings you out on a broad track just behind a row of almshouses.

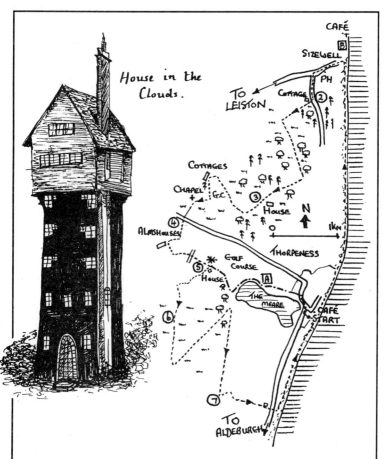

House in the
Clouds.

A. The House In The Clouds: When Ogilvie built Thorpeness as a holiday resort, he required a fresh water supply. He brought the post mill from Aldringham to pump the water from a well and disguised the water storage tank with a false house on a tower. A later house was built at the base among the supporting pillars.

B. The Suffolk Wildlife Trust, with the National Rivers Authority, has completed extensive dune reclamation work here, turning the badly eroded dunes back into both good sea defence and habitat.

Sea Holly

Turn left and, just before reaching the farm, bear left with the track until you reach a road. Cross and take the footpath opposite. Go over the meadow, heading towards the corner of a garden 50m or so to the left of a house.   ***

5. Turn right to pass the house and, after another 150m, take the footpath on your left. At a confusion of tracks, go straight ahead until the track forks when you reach a telegraph pole. Turn left to go downhill into the area of reedbeds and follow the boardwalk to Warren Heath.

6. Go straight ahead and, at the end of the path at the small car park, turn left to recross the heath. Shortly after you enter woodland, look out for a metal gate on your right to join the permissive path along the course of the old railway.

7. After passing through a metal gate on the railway walk, turn left to cross the water meadows back to the beach. Turn left and when you reach Thorpeness, go in front of the houses as far as the second boardwalk where you turn left to get back to the car park.   ***

*** SHORTCUT: After crossing the stile, turn left on the track and, when you come to the old level crossing gates, carry on ahead on the narrow path 15m to the left of overhead power lines. The path continues round the right hand edge of the golf course. As you near the clubhouse, take the track ahead between the House In The Clouds and the windmill to the road. Turn right and return to the car park.

WALK SIX

Around Aldeburgh

Aldeburgh's story, like so many of the towns on this coast, is one of a constant battle against and living from the sea. The Roman Town has long ago been washed away. Moot Hall is now on the edge of the beach to the North but it was once at the centre of the Tudor town, which means that half of that town's area has also been lost over the years.

A look at the church registers give some idea of the town's close association with the sea. Surnames like Carp, Crabbe, Pike, Sammon, Spratte, Turbette, Wale and Whiting can be found in abundance after a struggle with the spellings and old fashioned writing.

It was to the south of Aldeburgh that the worst lifeboat accident in Suffolk occurred, on the 7th of December 1899. The lifeboat "Aldeburgh", a Norfolk and Suffolk type boat built to answer the needs of the beachmen, was launched into a heavy sea in answer to the sound of guns over the water. Having gone southwards, the lifeboat then attempted to cross the inner shoal where it was met by a series of huge waves, the last of which rolled her firstly on to her side and then, as the masts broke, completely over. Some of the crew, including the coxwain, Charles Ward, who had replaced the legendary James Cable who was ill for this trip, managed to struggle free of the lifeboat, flinging themselves clear, and scramble ashore. Six men out of the crew of 18 were trapped under the 13 ton "Aldeburgh" as she turned over. The boat was driven on to the beach where frantic but unsuccessful efforts were made to lift her up and thus free the men underneath. The six men perished and one man died a few months later from the affects of the accident. The amazing bravery of the lifeboatmen was demonstrated a couple of months later when, in a replacement boat and again in heavy seas, many of the same men enacted a dramatic rescue of the steamer, Hylton, aground on Sizewell Bank.

It is also to the south of the town that the sea has made its most recent effort to break through. Not much exists at Slaughden now, just a couple of boat clubs and a track leading past the Martello

Tower to the remote Orfordness. In past centuries it was a port and shipbuilding centre with fishing boats going as far afield as Iceland and Norway. There was a thriving group of cottages, pubs, factories and warehouses. The last pub, The Three Mariners, was washed away in 1905 and the last house, the Marshman's Cottage, disappeared around 1920. It was at this point, during the great storm of early 1953, that for a short time the River Alde found a way into the sea, rather than continuing on its circuitous route past Orford to Shingle Street.

Just outside Aldeburgh, to the north, lies Thorpeness where the Meare is now popularly used as a boating lake. This was hand dug on the former site of Aldeburgh's northern harbour.

The Walk - 9.5km (6 miles)

Parking at the Slaughden end of the High Street gives you the opportunity, if you have timed your visit correctly, to sample the best fish and chips in Suffolk at the end of your walk. One of the delights of this walk is breasting the river bank opposite Stanny Point and feeling so isolated from the world at large yet, on turning, finding how close you are to the town. As with many of the other river walks, the vegetation can make the going difficult in mid-summer but normally the path at the foot of the bank is OK.

START: Park at the far end of the High Street either in the car park or out on the road. Make your way to the sea wall then turn left to head along the promenade towards Thorpeness.

2. Just before you reach the isolated bungalow between Aldeburgh and Thorpeness, turn left away from the seashore to cross water meadows.

3. On reaching rising ground, turn left to follow the course of the old railway on a permitted path towards Aldeburgh.

4. At the end of the railway path, near to the caravan park, go straight

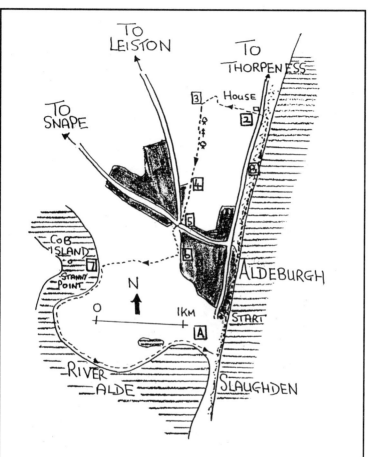

A. In the 17th century, salt was an important locally produced commodity all along the coast. The Aldeburgh salt pans were situated on the marshy area to the south of the town near Slaughden.

B. Amber is a yellowy-brown translucent fossil resin. Major deposits are found in the Baltic, and the tides and currents of the North Sea deposit small amounts on the Suffolk beaches - especially around Aldeburgh. The larger lumps often have wonderfully preserved fossilized insects trapped in the amber.

ahead, ignoring paths to your left and right.

5. When you get to the road, turn right then cross the road near the roundabout to take the track towards the fire station. At the playing field, cross to the far left hand corner.

6. Halfway along the allotments, take the gate on your right to cross into the water meadows. The path may be difficult to see at first but go straight ahead to cross a series of bridges and stiles and a sandy track to the river bank.

7. Turn left to follow the river wall all the way to Slaughden, then turn left back to the start. In summer it may be easier to walk at the foot of the river wall as it does become overgrown where it is not walked very often.

AVOCET

WALK SEVEN

Snape - Blaxhall Common - Tunstall Common - Tunstall Forest - Iken - Snape

Many of us will never forget the Great Storm of 16th of October 1987. We awoke to a relentless strong wind, seemingly trying to tear the world around us apart. Trees felled, sheds and greenhouses wrecked, electricity and telephone wires down, plus the occasional roof tile crashing around our ears.

One of the areas where the devastation was most apparent was Rendlesham and Tunstall Forest. Here, photographs show a scene of almost wartime destruction with large areas cleared and many trees brutally snapped off a few feet from the ground. In all, something like 700,000 trees were lost. This meant, of course, that there was much more wood than could be coped with by normal means. Approximately 13 years worth of timber was felled in just a few hours, leaving foresters with the enormous problem of disposing of it all. As there was far too much for normal factories to cope with, some had to be stored for later use. To keep wood in good condition it has to be continously sprinkled with water and some, ironically, was even exported to Sweden for processing into paper pulp.

In the immediate aftermath of the storm most people considered it to be an ecological disaster, but those able to stand back a little, and resist the temptation to start to clear and tidy too much, soon came to see the opportunity it presented. On inspection it was apparent that it was not the ancient woodlands that had suffered, but more recently planted and not so well established areas. Indeed, where big old trees had fallen, nature was only too ready to move in and establish a new and marvellous horizontal habitat alongside the old verticle one. New plants, fungi and insect life all began to flourish and, in places where light had been shut out for years, it allowed long dormant seeds to spring into life. Having marvelled at the wealth of bluebells in the last couple of years I am sure this is a consequence of the clearances that happened. Surely a natural regeneration of woodland is a much more sane response than any hasty and ill considered planting pro-gramme being put in place.

At Rendlesham and Tunstall, after the good wood was cleared, the debris was placed in a series of ridges, themselves a fine habitat for all sorts of small creatures, and areas have been replanted mainly with corsican pine, a much faster growing species than the original scots pine, at a thickness of 2,500 per hectare. In a few years time a new forest will have hidden much of the devastation of that wild October night.

The Walk - 15.5km (9.75 miles)
Shorter Walk is 10km (6.25 miles)

I have started this walk from Snape Maltings though alternative starts could be made from Tunstall Heath or Iken Cliff Car Park. This walk features what must be the best known view across a river anywhere in Suffolk. I defy anyone to stand at Iken Cliff and quietly look over the misty bay towards the church over the water and not to be moved by the experience. Refreshments are available at The Maltings either in the tea rooms or River Bar, or at the Plough and Sail public house.

START: At the front of the maltings, turn left on the main road to Woodbridge. After about 100m take the minor road on your right to Blaxhall. When you reach a road coming in from your right, take the track opposite into the woods. There are three parallel tracks here, all leading to your objective at the top of the hill, which is an old pit.
***

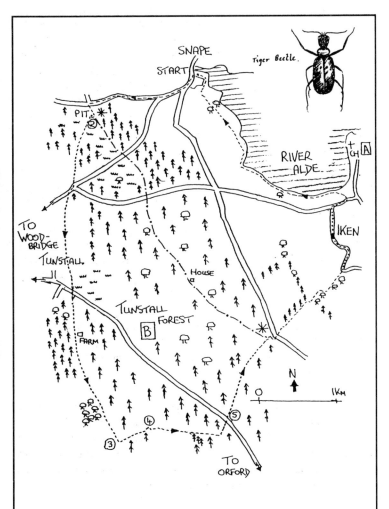

A. Iken is named after the Iceni tribe, best known for its queen, Boudica. The first church was set up on an island in the river by Botolph, a wandering preacher, in 654 A.D.

B. Tunstall forest is the only place in Suffolk where the White Admiral butterfly can be regularly seen.

2. Pass around the left of the pit to take the main path on the opposite side across the heath. Keep going straight ahead until a road is reached. Turn right and, just beyond the Iken Road, take the oblique track off to your left. This brings you to Tunstall Common and a confusion of tracks. Just keep straight on to the road, cross and go ahead on the track marked by telephone wires.

3. Follow this track for about 2km until you come to a pole gate on your left, across a ride marked by two red and white posts.

4. Take this ride and, at a crossway of marked paths, turn right and then left after about 70m. On reaching a broad track at a T-junction turn left to the road.

5. Cross and continue on the track. As this track reaches a gravel track go straight on. *** Just before you reach the road, turn right keeping the hedge on your left. After 100m, go through a waymarked gap in the hedge to the road.

6. Cross, then follow the path opposite along the field edge to a belt of trees. When this comes to an end, go to the right for a few metres then turn left and follow the edge of the wood, then a line of silver birches, to the road.

7. Turn left and, at the T-junction, right for 400m before taking the signposted path to Snape on your left. This path is generally easy to follow up the river, the only difficulty being as you reach a house on your left. Here you have to go up the slope a little way, then turn right to take the path by a small summer house, rather than continue on the river wall as it is broken ahead of you.

*** SHORTCUT: At the disused pit, carry on ahead on the track across the heath. Cross two roads and keep right on. When you come to a house, keep to the right of it to continue across the heath until you reach a substantial gravel track. Turn left and, just before you reach the road, turn right to rejoin the main path.

WALK EIGHT

Orford - Butley Ferry - Orford - Sudbourne - Orford

Although the river Stour, the South and the Dutch coasts have their Merman legends it is perhaps the Orford Merman that is the most well known. In the mid to late 1100s Orford still had a harbour facing into the open North Sea. It was then that local fishermen caught a wild man in their nets. Ralph of Coggeshall, a monk and chronicler, described him as being naked and hairy with a long beard and "being a man in all his members". He was taken into the castle where the custodian, Bartholemew de Glanville, made an attempt to get him to talk. He couldn't be persuaded to do this, or perhaps he was unable to do so, so he was tortured and hung by his feet but still he said nothing. He was taken to the castle chapel in the hope that he would show some reverence but did not do so. One version of events says that he would only eat fish, another that he ate all that was offered him, raw or cooked, while a third stated he "ate most ravenously, first squeezing the blood out with his strong hands". After several days he was returned to the harbour for some reason where, though guarded by three rows of nets, he escaped to the sea.

What could this Merman have been? Possibly a small walrus, a rarity on these shores, or just possibly a seal? It seems unlikely that local fishermen would not have recognised either though.

Orfordness has for ages been a mysterious and inaccessible place under the ownership of the Ministry of Defence and the Atomic Weapons Research Establishment (AWRE). Now purchased by the National Trust, it will soon be open for people to explore its secrets, including the pagoda like buildings visible from the town. Orfordness has been the site of various lighthouses and the first, in 1603, was made of wood and had a coal fire as a beacon, so it was not surprising that it burnt down.

The Military first came to Orfordness in 1915 in the shape of the Armament Experimental Flight of the Central Flying School, Royal Flying Corps. By 1916 the runway had been built and the first aircraft had arrived. Their work was mostly concerned with the testing of bombs and bomb sights and later with the development of fighter

43

planes and the parachute. It was a fighter from Orfordness that scored the one success in this country against a Zeppelin, which was brought down in a field near Theberton with only two survivors.

Between the wars the station was used as a satellite station for Martlesham Heath as well as being a firing and bombing range. In the late 1920s the first of many wireless masts appeared. With the outbreak of the Second World War it again became active and thus became a target for German bombers. In a raid on the 22nd of October, 1942, a Dornier bomber dropped its load on Orford Market Square and the council housing on the Town Farm Estate, killing 13 people. Later in the war, on the 29th March, 1945, gunfire from aircraft based at Orford destroyed the last flying bomb to approach the British Isles.

After the war the RAF took their leave, but experimentation continued with the Royal Aircraft Establishment and the AWRE testing, amongst other things, the triggers for atomic weapons. A joint British/American radio surveillance station, monitoring military radio communications behind the Iron Curtain, was operational for a few years after weapons testing finished.

Eventually though, this once isolated outpost was returned to its previous peaceful and deserted state and has remained so since.

The Walk - 18km (11.25 miles)
Shorter Walk is 10.5km (6.5 miles)

The section around Gedgrave Marshes is not a public footpath and can be missed if you prefer, though I have never been stopped whilst following the river wall. Park at the Quay car park and take your refreshment at one of the pubs or restaurants in the town. I like the Jolly Sailor myself, with its brass strip on the fireplace showing the level of the 1953 flood.

START: Walk down to the quay and turn right to follow the river wall around Chantry Point, as far as the footpath sign pointing inland. From here the river wall is no longer a right of way so, if you prefer, you can head inland to the road here but in doing so you will miss

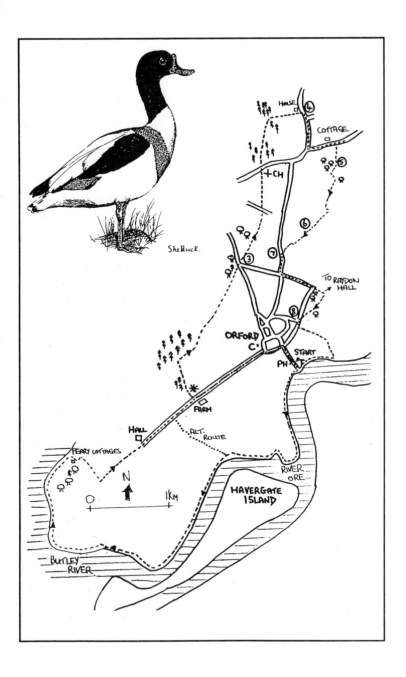

Shelduck.

HOUSE

COTTAGE

4

5

CH

6

7

3

TO RAYDON HALL

8

ORFORD C.

START

PH

FARM

ALT. ROUTE

HALL

FERRY COTTAGES

RIVER ORE

N

1KM

HAVERGATE ISLAND

BUTLEY RIVER

some fine river walking round to Butley Ferry. I carry on regardless.

2. On reaching Ferry Cottages turn right on a sandy track. When this track reaches another, turn left. This turns into a road at Gedgrave Hall. *** Just past a small postbox on your left, turn left on a sandy track. On reaching woods ahead of you, follow the track as it bears right.

3. Cross the road to a footpath on the far side. Cross another road and another at the church to enter woodland. At a crossing of paths, with thick woods ahead on your left and a small clump of straggly pines on your right, turn right to reach the road.

4. Turn right and take the second road on your left signposted to Crag Farm. 80m after passing a pink cottage on your left, take the footpath on your right. Go through a gate into a meadow and follow the drainage ditch on your left to a rough bridge.

5. Cross and go to your right over the meadow. After passing woods on your right go through a gate to a stile. Follow the obvious path, at first with a meadow on your left and then across open fields. At a

sandy track go left for 50m then right onto a bridleway.

6. Pass through an old iron gate and turn right for a few metres then left through a small gate. The bridleway seems to go through the middle of the field but it is normally easier to follow the right hand edge of the field to the road.

7. Turn left and left again at the crossroads. As the road turns right, carry on ahead on the road to Raydon Hall. At the end of the meadow, on your right, take the footpath across to the far corner into the woods. Cross a stile and a field to a house in the far corner.

8. At the road, turn left and after 80m left again on a well marked path to the river. When you get there, turn right to make your way back to the quay. ***

*** SHORTCUT: Continue down the road past Richmond Farm. Turn right when you come to the castle and right again as you meet the main road back to the quay.

Orford Castle.

WALK NINE

Boyton - Butley River - River Ore - Boyton - Butley - Burrow Hill - Boyton

"Crisp's Horse", as it is known, was foaled in 1768 by Thomas Crisp of Abbey Farm, Butley and it is from this horse that every pure bred Suffolk Punch can be traced.

The 'Punch' of Suffolk Punch has associations with Mr Punch of Punch and Judy fame. Like the horse, he was a short thick set fellow. Samuel Pepys says that fat children with short legs were called punches and it is from a combination of these factors that the name was transferred to the horse.

At the start of the Second World War there were still over 25,000 working horses of various sorts in Suffolk, ploughing, drilling, raking and carting but, with the coming of cheap oil and extensive mechanisation in the 1950s, this number rapidly declined to the very small number to be seen today.

The Suffolk stands around 16 hands high (although more recently some taller ones have been bred), has a large head and graceful appearance. It has a large stomach which was a definite asset when the typical working day for the horse was 6.30am to 2.30pm without a break to eat. A horse would easily consume a stone of oats and a stone of hay a day, with grass being the main food in summer and sometimes chopped roots in winter. One of the major assets of the horse is its lack of leg hair which was a great help on the heavy clay of High Suffolk. (Also useful in the First World War when it was used to drag guns in the mud and mire of the trenches of Europe because of its tremendous pulling power.) With the advent of hard roads in the fist part of the century it was found that the Suffolk, with its soft hooves, was unfit for much road work. Breeders were determined to deal with the problem, though, and a special class was developed at the various shows for foot quality. This proved so successful that it is probably better now in this area than most other breeds.

Suffolk has several Sorrel Horse pubs, with the colour sorrel describing the original reddish to yellowy brown of the Suffolk

Punch. Now all Suffolks are described as basically chesnut (note the lack of a middle t) but within this colouring are seven different shades ranging from brown-black mahogany through dull-dark, light-mealy, red, golden and lemon to bright chesnut. This last is by far the most popular. Normally there is a white star on the forehead or a thin blaze running down the front of the face.

Few studs remain today. One of the finest, where horses can be readily seen today from the adjoining footpath (Walk 10), is at Hollesley Bay Colony.

Suffolk Punch at work.

The Walk - 14.5km (9 miles)
Shorter Walk 1 is 9.5km (6 miles)
Shorter Walk 2 is 11km (6.75 miles)

Park in the RSPB car park at Banter's Barn Farm. This walk offers a fine variety of track, meadow and river walking. Refreshment is available at the recently re-opened Boyton Bell or, if the weather is fine, why not take a picnic up on to Burrow Hill.

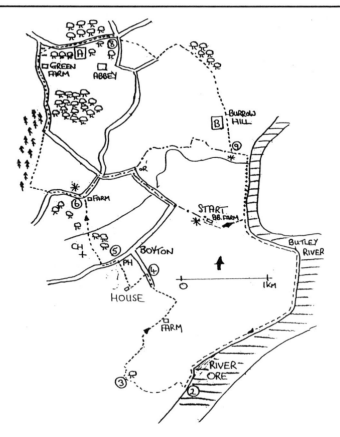

A. Butley Daffodil Woods are well worth a visit in the spring, giving a lovely display of early colour.

B. Burrow Hill was a Saxon settlement and cemetery. Hundreds of skeletons have been unearthed here, overwhelmingly male, suggesting either an army camp or a monastery. It was sited near the river as the boat was the easiest form of transport at that time. Originally an island linked to the mainland by a causeway, it was settled between 650 and 840 AD. Exposed as it was, it must have been very vulnerable to Viking raids.

START: Walk past the farm buildings and cross the meadows all the way to the river. Turn right and follow the river for 3km.

2. You need to be careful when looking for the point when you must leave the river bank. 200m after the river wall turns sharply left, a ramp comes in from your right. Walk along the ramp to a stile in the hedge. Do not cross but turn left through the meadows, keeping the hedge and ditch on your right.

3. After pasing through a wooden gate, you go gently uphill to meet a concrete track at a T-junction. Turn right and, after passing Boyton Hall Farm, turn left uphill on a sandy track when you come to the T-junction.

marsh Samphire .

4. A short while after the track becomes a road, take the footpath off to your left, following a track between hedges. Just before reaching the house at the end of the track, turn right to cross a field, then keep on down to the road.

5. Turn left and, at the Z-bend sign, turn right down a track. As the track forks by a large willow, go to your right to a metal gate, a wooden fence and stile and a grassy track beyond. At the meadow, keep straight ahead to a wooden bridge, then follow the right hand edge of the field to a small

Sea Pink.

paddock, then through a garden to the road. ***

6. Turn left and, when the road turns to the left after 400m, go ahead on the footpath. At the end of the field, turn right on first a track and then a road.

7. 100m after passing Green Farm on your right, turn right on a track. On rejoining the road, turn right again and continue to the crossroads.

8. At the crossroads, turn right and, after 25m, take the footpath along a track to your left. At the rough road, turn left and, at the T-junction of tracks, turn right to pass woodland on your left, then cross a field to climb Burrow Hill.

9. After crossing over the hill, turn left to the river bank. *** Turn right for 1km to leave the bank where you first joined it (100m before the red brick building on the shoreline). Cross the meadows back to Banter's Barn Farm.

*** SHORTCUT: Having passed close to the house and emerged on the road, turn right and, at the cross-roads, turn right again. At the next bend you have the choice of staying on the road and continuing in a straight line back to the start, or of taking the track to Ferry Farm and crossing meadows to the river bank.

Short Eared
Owl.

WALK TEN

Alderton - Shingle Street - Hollesley Bay -
Shingle Street - Alderton

Martello Towers are prominent all along the east coast from Shoreham-on-Sea in Sussex up to Slaughden, and can be seen on the walks at Felixstowe Ferry, Shingle Street and Aldeburgh.

In 1794, a Royal Naval Squadron under Lord Hood was supporting Corsican insurgents who came up against French revolutionaries and besieged them in a fortified tower at Cape Mortella. (The lovely sounding cape where the myrtles grow.) So sturdy was this tower that a small force of 30 men was able to repel three British frigates and, when the British returned with 1400 men, they were only able to take the tower when a chance shot set it on fire. In 1803, with the threat of imminent French invasion, the Duke of York, who was Commander in Chief, ordered a string of forts to be built along the coast, replicating most of the features of the Cape Mortella tower. His version was egg-shaped, with the sharper end pointing seaward to deflect incoming shell fire. The walls on the seaward side were about 9ft thick and most towers contained around 700,000 bricks. The larger redoubts at Slaughden and Dovercourt held over 1,000,000 bricks. Surrounded by a ditch and 30-40ft high, access was gained by a ladder leading to a door about 20ft up the rear wall. The main armament was a 24lb swivel gun, designed to deal with approaching ships, with two 5.5 inch Howitzers to fire on any invading troops, should they manage to make a landing.

You would imagine that they should be known as Mortella Towers, but it appears that an Admiralty clerk somehow managed to transpose the 'o' and the 'a' so, ever since, we have known them as Martello Towers. Napoleon, of course, never invaded, so perhaps the towers had some deterrent effect. The French dubbed them "bulldogs" but the local population referred to them more scathingly as "Mr Pitt's Pork Pies".

After the end of the Napoleonic Wars the threat of invasion receded and the towers were used as an invaluable aid in the battle against smuggling by acting as a long chain of look out towers.

The Walk - 14km (8.75miles)
Shorter Walk is 10km (6.25 miles)

Park, if possible, in Alderton High Street. The pub in Alderton does serve food in summer, but why not sit on the beach at Shingle Street with a picnic, enjoying the terns diving for fish in the river mouth.

START: The walk starts at the corner of the Hollesley road near Don's Store and the butchers'. A signpost reading "Shingle Street 2 miles" takes you down a cinder track. The path really is very easy to follow to the sea wall, so I won't insult you with further directions. Just keep going.

2. At the sea wall I normally abandon the footpath to cross to the edge of the sea and turn left to walk towards Shingle Street, heading up the beach again at the cottages. Tiring on the loose stones, but it is only for a short while.

> **B.** The plant communities that have managed to colonise parts of the shingles are greatly influenced by the length of time the shingle has remained undisturbed and the amount of fine particles, both organic and inorganic, that have accumulated between the pebbles. It is probably best therefore to keep clear of areas of the beach where plants are growing.

3. Walk along past the front of the cottages, then follow the path either on or by the river wall. When this turns away from the main river, follow it inland until you reach the road. ***

4. Turn right to cross the bridge and go over the stile on your right to take the path back on the other riverbank. When you reach a strip of concrete river wall, turn left inland, passing through a gate onto a track.

5. At the road, turn left at the signpost for Hollesley and Shingle Street. Go uphill and, 100m after turning the corner, take the concrete track on your left. At the road, go straight ahead, then round the corner back to the bridge. ***

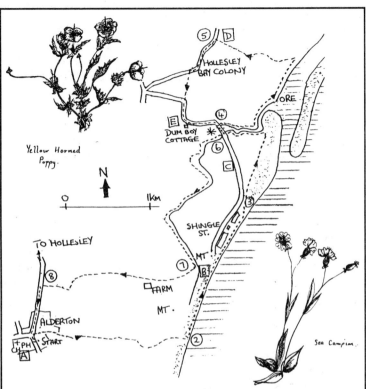

Yellow Horned Poppy.

N

0 ————— 1 KM

TO HOLLESLEY

ALDERTON

Sea Campion.

A. Poverty and low church attendance have long been a feature of the Suffolk countryside. Some time ago the Rector of Alderton helped the poor of the parish with bowls of soup, but only on the condition that they had attended church the previous Sunday.

C. Before the road across the Oxley Marshes was built, the only access to Shingle Street was along the beach from Bawdsey.

D. Suffolk Punch horse collection at Hollesley Bay Colony.

E. Dumboy Cottage was named after the inhabitant who, being dumb, was able to keep watch for the customs men on behalf of the local smugglers, but was impervious to their questioning.

6. You now have a choice as to which river bank to follow. They are equally easy/difficult, depending on the state of the vegetation (which includes brambles and hawthorn bushes). You may sometimes be forced from the crown of the bank. I normally take the concrete track to the pump house and cross to the far side of the river, via the steps on the sluice gate.

7. You are now following the river upstream, towards the Martello Tower at Shingle Street. As you approach the seashore again, find a stile on your right leading to a path across a field, following the line of telephone poles. Follow this until you reach a track heading to the farm.

8. Continue along the track until you reach the road; here you turn left, back into Alderton and your starting point.

*** SHORTCUT: The shortest short cut of all. When you come to the road crossing Oxley Marshes for the first time, cross and rejoin the main path at the pumping station.

Martello Tower.

WALK ELEVEN

Shottisham - Ramsholt - Stonner Point - Methersgate - Sutton Hall - Shottisham

This walk along the Deben from Ramsholt to Methersgate is one of the jewels in the crown of Suffolk walking. Perhaps because it is difficult in one or two places, it reveals areas rarely seen. Apart from in the Ramsholt area, you seldom meet a soul and it is a real delight to sit at Stonner Point and look across to the busy little village of Waldringfield and yet feel almost alone in the world.

The Ramsholt Arms was converted from the old Ferryman's cottage and is one of the few pubs you will find that has no pub sign. The shelters at the bottom of the garden were one of the first signs of the leisure industry arriving on the Deben. At the turn of the century visitors would come by horse and carriage to take afternoon tea by the river here. This was the scene of a tragic incident when, in February 1945, an American Flying Fortress took off from Debach Airfield intending to bomb Nurnberg railway yards. Unfortunately, an engine caught fire and the pilot had to try and ditch the plane in the Deben. Sadly eight of the crew perished, though the pilot escaped.

As you move up river, you reach the area near Sluice Cottage, known as The Rocks because this part of the river has a rocky bottom. The rock is Septaria which was used in the building of Orford Castle. Cattle used to be swum across the river here on their way to Ipswich market.

The 'Tips', for all their lonely beauty, are not a natural feature, but were made as a result of part of a land reclamation project of over 100 years ago. Robert Cobbold was attempting to reclaim some 150 acres of land from the river for farming but was stopped by Trinity House who feared his scheme would interfere too much with the tidal flow of the river. The flat topped Scots Pines hold a long established heronry and it is well worth stopping here and watching for a while.

Nowadays, landing places along the rivers are often known as 'Hards'. In the past they were often known as 'Gates', from the Norse word meaning a way to the shore over the water. Methersgate is one example of the use of the word, as are Shotley Gate and

Havergate. Another word for landing place is 'Stone', from the Suffolk word for gravel or flint. Surprisingly this word seems to have survived more in Essex, with places like Mersea Stone and St Osyth's Stone, than in Suffolk. There is now no sign of Guston Stone, which is the part of Kirton Creek from where the river ferry started. I wonder if Stonner Point also has some connection with this derivation.

The Walk - 16km (10 miles)
Shorter Walk is 12km (7.5 miles)

This is one of my favourite walks. The best place to park is in the small car park in front of the church, or on the road in front of the pub. It has some of the best river walking around, though the path can be difficult to follow at The Tips and at Lodge Plantation. Refreshment is available at the Shottisham Sorrel Horse, or overlooking the river at the Ramsholt Arms.

Long Tailed Duck

START: Make your way to The Sorrel Horse and take the broad track opposite. Just after 1km you come to a road: cross and take the road opposite. As this road turns sharply left, turn right on a track which soon bears left following telephone poles.

2. After passing fields, pheasant pens and more fields on your left, take a track, just past a hedge, towards Ramsholt church. At the church, take the path straight ahead, down a gully. Go through a gate into meadowland, where the path bears right, then left to the river wall.

3. Turn left here if you want to visit the Ramsholt Arms, or right if you want to continue the walk. You are now following the river for 6.5km to Methersgate Quay. Walking either on or beside the river wall, or on the beach, the going is generally easy but there are two problem areas. Firstly at Lodge Plantation where, if the tide is high, it is easier to follow the path through the wood to the field edge, then turn left to walk along this, towards Sluice Cottage. Secondly, near The Tips and Nettle Hill, where you may have to clamber up the bank to find the path through the woods. The point of access to the beach which should be taken is where, after leaving Stonner Point, the path leaves the river on the short cut. *** As the path runs away from the shore, turn left down the river bank, behind the reedbed. If this all sounds complicated, don't despair, plough onwards upriver somehow - it really is well worth it!

4. You know you have reached Methersgate when you come to a house and quay. Start inland on the track, then cross into the first meadow on your right, either by the fence at the corner or, if it hasn't become overgrown, by the stile in the corner towards the cottage. Go to the far corner (the right hand edge) and cross the stile into woods. At the far end of the woods, go over another stile and follow the right hand edge of the meadow to another stile; cross, then turn left to bring yourself back to the track to Methersgate Hall.

5. Turn right and, at the Hall, go through the wicket gate onto the driveway. Follow this round to the right after 200m, into a long straight country lane. 200m after the road swings to the left at Cliff Farm, take the track off to the right.

6. At a T-junction, turn right, then left, then left again to pass around the field. Having done this, turn right and continue until you reach the road. *** Turn left and, on reaching Sutton Hall, right.

7. At the next junction, turn left and, after passing the hotel on your right, you reach the main road.

8. Cross here then take the path diagonally to your left, to a concrete

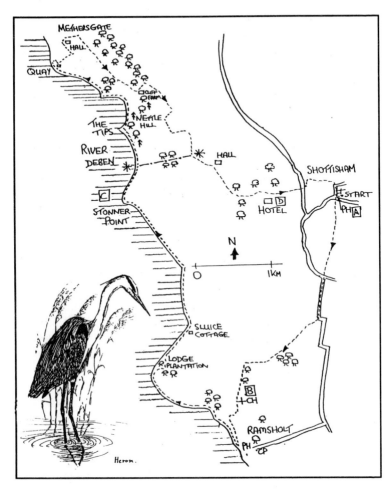

Heron.

bridge over the stream. Cross and aim for the right hand side of the allotments ahead. Follow the hedge on your right for a short while and, where a road is seen on your right, go through a gap and along the road back to your starting point.

*** SHORTCUT: As the track leads away from the river after you leave Stonner Point, follow it past Lower Farm to rejoin the main path coming in from your left as you approach Sutton Hall.

A. The Sorrel Horse had a smuggler's hiding place in a cellar which has now been converted into a living room.

B. Ramsholt Church Tower was originally a Saxon watchtower on the lookout for Danish raiders coming up the Deben. From the top of the tower the whole area, from Felixstowe Ferry to Woodbridge, can be surveyed. The churchyard here is one of several in the county maintained by the Suffolk Wildlife Trust for its conservation value.

Ramsholt Church.

C. In the exceptionally cold winter of 1963 the river froze, allowing the inhabitants of Waldringfield to walk all the way across to Stonner Point.

D. Wood Hall Hotel: A young girl staying at the hotel at the start of this century fell into the lake and was drowned. Her ghost can be seen and heard roaming an upper corridor, searching for her parents and bouncing a tennis ball. In the grounds there is also the ghost of a stallion which strangled itself on a hitching post.

WALK TWELVE

Sutton Hoo - Methersgate - Sutton - Sutton Heath - Sutton Hoo

In the early Sixth Century, Wuffa, from Uppland in Sweden, and his family crossed the North Sea and started a dynasty in East Anglia. His grandson, Raedwald, was King of Eastern England, south of the Humber, and he ruled from a palace at Rendlesham. It is probable that he was buried at the royal burial ground at Sutton Hoo in AD624 or 625.

The first proper excavation of the 19 mounds at Sutton Hoo was undertaken in 1939 by Basis Brown, with the assistance of the gardener and gamekeeper of Mrs Pretty, the owner of the site. Luckily, they were able to decipher traces of a large longship buried there and enlisted the help of, firstly, Ipswich Museum and then Charles Philips of Cambridge University. It was he who unearthed the burial chamber in the centre of the ship, containing all an Anglo-Saxon king could need for his journey into the next life. Raedwald, although supposedly converted to Christianity in AD620, was known to retain many pagan ideals. In his palace he had two altars - one to the Christian god and one to his pagan gods.

Mound One, which was 12ft high and 100ft long, where the ship was found, is a truly remarkable discovery. The ship, a double ended clinker built boat, was almost 90ft long, 14ft wide, had seating for 38 oarsmen, and a wooden burial chamber in the middle which would have been hung with fine tapestries. Although no body was found in the highly acidic ground, soil changes indicate that a body was once buried there, and this is confirmed by the presence of iron coffin fittings. Here were found 41 precious objects, including classical spoons, silver from Eastern Europe and magnificent goldwork by local craftsmen. The discovery of weapons such as a sword, javelin, spears and the man's helmet and shield show that he was a warrior, and the bowls, spoons, large drinking horn and cauldron were to supply his bodily needs in the next world.

The reason why this mound survived unrobbed, where so many others were pillaged, seems to be that one end of the mound was ploughed away at one stage. When grave robbers dug down into what they considered to be the centre of the grave they missed, luckily, and this amazing treasure survived. If you want to get some idea of what was found here, replicas of many of the objects can be seen on display in Ipswich Museum.

Later excavations on and around the site have turned up a wealth of archaeological detail. Numerous 'sandmen' have been discovered. This is where the acidic soil has reacted with the bodies to leave perfect shapes in the sand with darker colours and different textures so the shape of each body can be carefully isolated from the surrounding area. In 1991, a grave of what is thought to be a young prince and his horse was discovered, complete with sword, shield, spear and decorated bridle. In Mound 17, and around Mound 6, were found the graves of human sacrifices and one man who was buried with what was, presumably, his most important possession - his plough.

Corsican Pine

The Walk - 13km (8 miles)

The best place to park for this walk is on the rough ground at the junction of the Hollesley and Bawdsey roads as you come from Woodbridge. The only slight problem on the walk is finding a path up Ferry Cliff. A short detour in Sutton takes you to The Plough for refreshment.

START: Cross the main road and take the broad track signposted to Sutton Hoo. Follow this to the excavation, carrying straight on to the pedestrian entrance to the site.

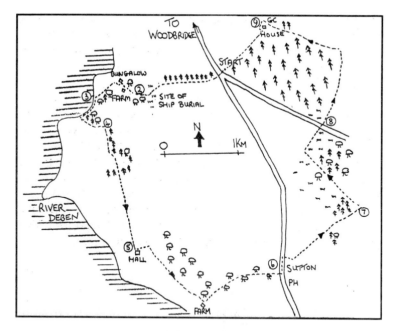

2. Turn right and go down the hill, passing to the right of the farm at the bottom. Almost immediately after a right turn in the track, turn left to pass a barn and bungalow on your right. Cross a stile and follow the right hand edge of the wood to the river bank.

3. Turn left and, when you reach the somewhat ramshackle steps, you have the choice of climbing here or continuing on the sometimes rather squelchy foreshore. Whichever you choose, you eventually reach a turf field; turn left to follow the edge of this field.

4. Turn right to follow a narrow band of woodland before crossing a field to a lane. You now carry on in an almost straight line until you reach Methersgate Hall.

5. Pass behind the buildings and find the small gate in the fence to your left, in front of the Hall. Go through and follow the lane, swinging right after around 200m. This takes you to Sutton.

6. At the main road, turn left and, after 300m, right onto a track. After a further 150m, turn left on a wide track.

7. At the end of a rather ugly RAF compound on your right, turn left to cross Sutton Common. At the end of a long track you reach a five bar gate, turn right here to reach the main road near Woodbridge Airfield.

8. Cross and carry straight on. At the end of woodland, turn left and, when you reach the golf course, turn right, then left, to pass through trees until you draw level with a bungalow.

9. Pass to the right of the bungalow, then turn left to cross over the fence to the path. Turn right and, when you approach the car park, veer off on to the sandy drive on your right for the last few metres to avoid a short stretch of busy road.

SHORTCUT: I hunted high and low for a short cut which pleased me, but eventually had to give up.

The Woodbridge Tide Mill, on the far side of the river
between points 2 and 3 on the walk.

WALK THIRTEEN

Waldringfield - Hemley - Kirton Creek -
Newbourne - Waldringfield

It was realised as long ago as the 18th Century that there was some value in spreading the red crag, which can be seen exposed on many of the riverside cliffs of the Deben and Orwell, on the poor quality land of the area. It originally acted as an acidity corrector to the soil but in the early 1840s J S Henlow, Professor of Minerals at Cambridge and Vicar of Hitcham, realised that the coprolites which were found in the crag had a high phosphate value. A boom industry exploiting this fact soon developed.

The word 'coprolite' comes from the Greek words meaning dung and stone and, difficult as it is to believe, this is just what coprolite is: fossilised dinosaur dung. The large sea going animals in the area in prehistoric times consumed vast amounts of plant material and smaller animals, then deposited their waste on the ocean bed. When these dinosaurs died, their bodies also fell to the bottom and all this matter formed a rich layer of phosphatic material which, at some much later time, was pushed up to its present position much nearer the surface.

Mills were opened to exploit this resource at Snape, Bramford and Ipswich which, by the late 1870s, were dealing with around 10,000 tons of coprolite a year. This amply demonstrates how important the industry must have become to the local economy. It is the explanation for many of the disused pits which litter the area for, as the coprolite became scarcer, the miners had to dig deeper and deeper. Some attempt was made to dig shafts, as in coal mining, but this proved too dangerous and uneconomic. By the end of the century the whole industry was probably on its last legs anyway, as enormous quantities of easily mined phosphates were discovered in the guano deposits of South America. There was a short revival when trade routes were blocked in World War I and some efforts were made to spread crag as a fertiliser in the agricultural depression of the 1930s.

Waldringfield was one of the main areas of extraction, with over 1,000 tons being taken from the fields behind the Maybush Inn. This was processed down on the beach as a large amount of red crag had to be washed away from the coprolite nodules before they were usable. They were then loaded onto barges, sailed down the Deben, then back up the Orwell to Ipswich where the dungstone was ground at the mill. In the 1860s coprolite was so valuable that the vicar was able to sell enough from the glebe lands to repair his decaying church. The villagers of Waldringfield were able to sell whatever amounts they found in their gardens for large amounts of money, sometimes equalling their annual wage.

One final twist to the tale is that it was at Levington that the value of spreading crag on the fields was first realised and, after many amalgamations, the major agrichemical firm to emerge from the coprolite boom was Fisons. Fisons, to complete the neat circle, now has its research station in the village.

Silver Birch.

The Walk - 13.5km (8.5 miles)
Shorter Walk 1 is 7km (4.5 miles)
Shorter Walk 2 is 11km (6.75 miles)

Park in the public car park behind the Maybush in Waldringfield where refreshment is available, as it is at the Fox in Newbourne (cream teas at weekends in the summer!). Just one problem with this lovely walk: a short stretch as you approach Newbourne Springs where, in midsummer, the bracken does grow extremely high. The short cut can be used both ways. I think the best way is to park at the church at Hemley (Point 3), and return on the short cut from Newbourne (Point 11).

START: Walk down to the foreshore past the pub. Turn right to walk downstream and, when you reach the beach huts, turn right and head inland. After passing the large pond, turn left to cross an open field.

2. After passing a large house, turn right up a bridleway. On reaching the lodge, turn left to follow a concrete track across fields and past a farm. This eventually becomes a road leading to Hemley Church. ***

3. At the church, turn left towards the river. When you reach a gate after the last house, turn left along a footpath which bears right to take you downstream to Kirton Creek.

4. At the top of Kirton Creek, make your way down to the adjoining track. Continue up the gentle slope to a T-junction; turn right. As this track bears left towards a farm, go straight ahead, over a fence. (There is a stile hidden in the brambles in the corner.)

5. Go ahead through the meadow and, after passing through the metal farm gate, go right to pass through the farm buildings before taking the track ahead, passing just to the right of the house. At the corner, go straight ahead on the narrow footpath. This path winds through fields, becoming first a wider track, then a bridleway, and then it

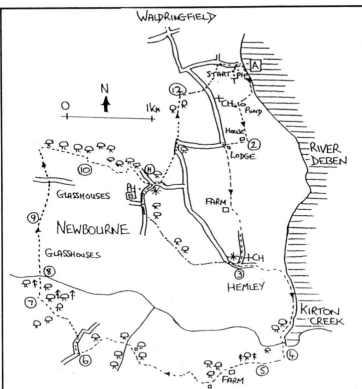

A. In the ceiling of the Maybush is a 'twizzler'. It was used by the barge skippers to decide whose turn it was to buy the drinks and, at Christmas, to gamble for the prize of a pig.

B. Newbourne was the home of the Suffolk giants, George and Meadows Page. In 1868 the brothers, George (7ft 7ins) and Meadows (7ft 5ins), went to Woodbridge Easter Fair where, at a sideshow, a tall man held a guinea above his head and challenged allcomers to reach up and take it. Unsurprisingly, George was able to, and took the man's place in the fair. The brothers married the same woman: first George married Kat Ewing, then he died and was replaced by Meadows. Kat was a very small lady, in contrast to the brothers, and she kept a shop in Newbourne for many years.

reaches a road.

6. Turn right, then after 250m, turn left to follow a field edge on your left. At the track at the bottom of the field, turn left and follow this track as it swings round to the right to follow the edge of woods on your right.

7. Take the track as it goes right into woods. This is sometimes marked by a disgusting gamekeeper's gibbet on the fence to your left as you turn. Nearing the bottom of the wood, the track swings right into an open field, but you go straight ahead, through the wood to a bridge over the river.

8. Cross the bridge, then the meadow to the far corner, not forgetting the lone stile in the middle. Cross the stile in the corner and turn right to pass to the right of the house ahead. Go over the road and up a concrete drive to a white gate.

9. This old green lane takes you to the road, which you cross to take the footpath slightly to your left. Follow this until you near woodland on your right: here there is a gap in the fence where the path goes off to follow the edge of the woods towards Newbourne. (This section, for about 150m, can become covered with high bracken in midsummer but the more people who are brave enough to walk it at this time the better it will become!)

10. After running along the edge of the wood for a while, the path does a dog leg to the right, then crosses the hedge, via a stile on your left, to follow the right hand edge of a field, downhill to a track going to your right at the bottom. After 300m, turn left into the SWT reserve of Newbourne Springs. On meeting another path, turn right and follow this to emerge on the road near the information centre in the old pump house.

11. Turn right and, at the junction *** turn left for 75m, then take the footpath on your left at the corner, passing through the old coprolite pit, up the slope, and across open fields. Turn left at the road and,

when the road turns sharply right, carry straight on across the field until you reach a long thin line of scrub.

12. Enter this scrub - I saw a fox ahead of me on the path one day - and, after 200m, turn right and cross the fields and road until you reach the houses on the edge of Waldringfield. Turn left down the lane, then right down the road, back to your starting point.

*** SHORTCUTS:

1. Turn right at Hemley church and, as the road turns right after 200m, take the track straight ahead. Follow the field edge as you go downhill past woods on your right, to a metal gate, and go through this into a meadow. The path runs parallel to the right edge of the meadow and about 15m away from it. After passing through trees, go downhill to cross the stream at a patch of scrubby trees. After crossing boggy ground, the path climbs and emerges near the village hall. Turn right and walk past the pub to rejoin the main path at the road junction.

2. The walk can alternatively be started at Hemley church and the short cut be done returning from Newbourne. At the T-junction, turn right and go past the Fox. Turn left at the village hall and go down to the bottom right of the field behind. Follow the path over the stream and bear right to cross the meadow, trees and then meadow, to the far left corner. Go through the gate and keep the hedge and woods on your left. Keep on to join a track and then a road to go straight ahead to the church.

Oyster Catcher.

WALK FOURTEEN

Felixstowe Ferry - Falkenham - Kirton Creek -
Felixstowe Ferry

The basic ingredients of a dangerous North Sea flood are a high tide, a weather system combining an area of high pressure over the Atlantic and a fierce and deepening depression crossing the North Sea. This causes a steep pressure gradient (loads of isobars on the weather chart) between the high and low pressure, leading to Northerly gales sweeping down the North Sea. The low barometric pressure can allow the level of the sea to rise several inches while, in dangerous contrast, the high pressure in the Atlantic is forcing the ocean level down, sending a surge of water both up the English Channel and also round the top of Scotland. This build up is made worse as the water is driven southwards by the hurricane winds, towards the narrow neck of the Straights of Dover, leading to an enormous build up of water in the southern North Sea.

So it was that on the night and day of 31st January and the 1st of February, 1953, that these conditions were fulfilled and an enormous surge of water swept inland from the Humber estuary, southwards. In Suffolk, the first effects were felt at Southwold. Very quickly the town became an island and remained so for the next two days. The piecemeal developments along Ferry Road were originally intended as holiday homes but, with the housing shortage after the war, had become permanently occupied throughout the year. They were inundated under an avalanche of water, many were totally wrecked and some were lifted bodily by the flood and carried along before being torn asunder after coming into crashing contact with more permanent objects. Southwards swept the surge, flooding the lower parts of Dunwich, near the church and school, and breaking the banks of the Alde, Ore, Deben and Orwell. In all, over 8,000 hectares of Suffolk land were flooded, some of which, especially along the Deben, were never returned to agricultural use. At Aldeburgh, for a short time, the sea wall at Slaughden was broken, allowing the river Alde free access to the sea at that point for the first time for hundreds of years.

And so on to Felixstowe, the scene of the greatest loss of life. Just inland from the Orwell northern river bank lies Langer Road, Stour Avenue and Orwell Road. In 1953 the area contained many prefabricated buildings so, when the river wall gave way, there was little hope for many of the families living there. The final horrendous total came to 39 lives lost.

Will it happen again? Yes, the evidence is there. As East Anglia slowly sinks and, as global warming makes sea levels rise, the risk increases year by year. A much improved flood warning system and better communications, added to higher quality housing in the most vulnerable areas, probably means a lower death toll next time. The government and water authorities were faced with a stark choice. They could invest huge amounts of money in an enormous concrete barrier around the coast, and in so doing destroy the character of our lovely shoreline. The option they chose was to provide adequate protection for the main centres of population and allow the less populated areas to bear the brunt of the next flood, when it comes.

The Walk - 15km (9.5 miles)
Shorter Walk 1 is 11km (6.75 miles)
Shorter Walk 2 is 8km (5 miles)

Parking and refreshment for this walk are available at the Victoria Inn, Ferryboat Inn and the Ferry Cafe. If you are not in the mood for a really long stretch of river bank walking, a shorter walk starting and finishing at Falkenham Church, via Kirton Creek, is a good idea.

START: Take the path between the inn and the cafe to the river wall. Follow this as far as The King's Fleet (lkm).

2. Take the track just past The King's Fleet, heading inland. This becomes a road just past Deben Lodge Farm. Take the road to Kirton which appears on your right.

3. Almost opposite a road on your right, take the footpath on your left, cutting across a field towards the church. As you rejoin the road, turn left, then almost immediately right along a track.

A. The seals which can be sometimes seen on the sandbanks around the mouth of the Deben and along the river were rescued by the Norfolk Seal Sanctuary at the time of the seal virus and returned here when well. Life is so good living off fishermens' waste that the seals are most reluctant to leave the area. If you are really lucky, you may see the bottle nosed dolphin that visits the mouth of the river occasionally.

B. The chain ferry which used to cross to Bawdsey from here was installed by Sir Cuthbert Quilter of Bawdsey Manor. Although it was available for use by the public, it had to return immediately to the bank if a Quilter family car appeared on either side, no matter how far across on its journey it happened to be.

C. Kirton Creek is now a very quiet backwater and one of my favourite places on the river. I first came here one perfect cold February morning. Sun spangled beads of ice sparkled on the dead heads of last years cow parsley, the frost was hard in the ground and there was a bright sheen of ice on the river, reflecting the low morning sun.

In 1880 a dock was built here to serve the brickyard in the fields behind. Barges brought in horse muck to spread on the fields around until the mid 1930s. The remains of the barge 'Three Sisters' can still be seen at low tide, protruding from the mud. The crew had walked off her and gone home, declaring the boat to be in an unseaworthy state.

D. The lost port of Goseford covered the area from the mouth of the river up to Kirton Creek and inland as far as Falkenham and Kirton. Before the river was tamed, by the building of banks, it would have been a vast stretch of water almost three miles wide. Ships from here would have been very important in pursuing the wool trade with the near continent. With royal ownership of the manor of Walton, it became an assembly point for foriegn expeditions. Edward III gathered 13 ships with 300 seamen to carry him across to France and the Lowlands.

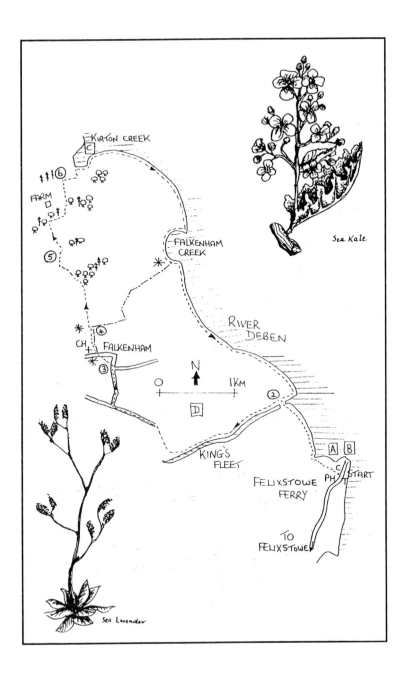

KIRTON CREEK
C

FARM

5

CH
FALKENHAM
3

KItON CREEK

FALKENHAM
CREEK

RIVER
DEBEN

N

O ———|——— 1KM

D

2

A B
C
Felixstowe Ferry PH START

To
FELIXSTOWE

Sea Kale

Sea Lavender

4. After about 300m, the track meets another track coming in from your right. Unless you want to take the shortcut, *** your path kinks left, then right, to carry on ahead.

5. At the T-junction of tracks, turn right and, after 150m, left, to directly cross an open field to a small gap in the trees at the far side. At the wood edge, turn right and, at the end of the wood, go through the hedge. Turn left to follow the edge of the field. At the corner, go straight ahead to join a track passing to the left of thin woodland.

6. At the T-junction, turn right and, after 250m, left, down to Kirton Creek. When you reach the creek, turn right and follow the river wall *** back to Felixstowe Ferry.

*** SHORTCUTS:

1. Turn right at the T-junction and head towards the river. When the path forks, take the left fork and, when the path reaches the river, turn right, back to the ferry.

2. Start at Falkenham Church and take the track leading to sections 4, 5 and 6 of this walk. On your way back along the river bank, turn right to take the track inland, just past Falkenham Creek. Having gone uphill, bear right as a track comes in from your left and turn left when you rejoin your earlier path to make your way back to the church.

WALK FIFTEEN

Searson's Farm - Trimley Reserve - Levington - Searson's Farm

In 1984, the Felixstowe Dock Company wanted to expand its port facilities up river to cover the Fagbury mudflats. As a result of protracted negotiations with the Suffolk County Council, the port agreed to provide 208 acres of adjacent land, formerly owned by Trinity College, Cambridge, to be developed as a nature reserve. In 1989 Trimley Reserve was opened and has since been managed by the Suffolk Wildlife Trust.

The ooze and saltings on the Orwell are internationally important as a winter feeding ground for waders and wildfowl from the arctic and sub-arctic. The foreshore habitat can only support a limited number of birds so that, as each area is filled in, the number of birds decreases. Fagbury mudflats only accounts for 7% of the intertidal mudflat of the Orwell but, even in harsh winter conditions, it remains relatively frostfree so a disproportionate number of birds feed there. Up to 80% of the oystercatchers, 41% of the dunlin, 40% of the ringed plover and 36% of the grey plover used it as their feeding grounds.

Under the agreement entered into between the dock company and the objectors to the bill presented to parliament, widespread landscaping of the area took place, including the planting of 500,000 trees. There was also the provision for 60% of the running costs of the reserve, up to a maximum of £15,000 per annum, to be paid for the next 30 years. The total cost of these measures is in the region of £2,000,000.

There is, of course, no way that a reserve on farmland at Trimley marshes can replace an area of mudflats and saltmarsh actually on the river. It is a bit like replacing your favourite cat with a rabbit: not the same. The site can, however, be developed into an important wildlife area on what was intensely farmed land. The hope is to provide a mixed habitat of permanent fresh water lagoons, with shingle scrapes fringed by reedbeds, a reservoir to maintain water levels and to flood adjacent areas of meadowland at different times of the year. All this is to be viewed from a series of well placed hides.

A vast amount of labour has already gone into the site. The 400 tons of ballast required to cover the shingle islands had to be spread by hand. 95,000 cubic metres of clay had to be removed and the top-soil replaced. A shelf was built along the reservoir wall to help plants colonise the area. New drainage ditches had to be dug, pits were excavated to provide cliff faces for sand martins, and the perimiter was surrounded by electric fencing to deter foxes. Finally, in 1992, a visitor centre was opened.

These herculean efforts soon bore fruit. By 1990, redshank were breeding on the reserve and, by 1991, nationally important numbers of teal were present. Among the many other birds to be seen are short eared owl, Brent geese, ringed plover, little tern and tufted duck. Rarities include black winged stilt, pectoral and stilt sandpipers and spoonbills. Not bad for what was sterile farmland a few years ago.

During 1995, the Felixstowe dock company started the last stage of the project. A huge bund, or bank, covered in trees is being created which will separate the greatly contrasting areas - the noisy bustling docks and the quiet, peaceful reserve.

Little Tern.

The Walk - 18km (11.25 miles)
Shorter Walk is 9km (5.5 miles)

A fine walk, with the Ship Inn at Levington conveniently situated at half way. Parking is available at Searson's farm. The only problem can be in finding the path through the second half of the marina but, as long as you remember you are following the riverbank upstream, you should not go wrong.

START: Follow the well marked track towards the nature reserve. Continue along the river bank, past the reserve *** and, after keeping the lakes on your right, enter the woods above the marina.

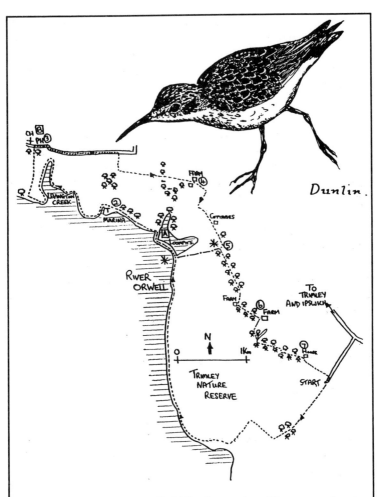

Dunlin.

A. The lakes here are called The Loompits. They were dug to extract the fertile loam which was spread on the fields around.

B. The 'Ship' at Levington, not surprisingly given its position close to the river, is one of the many Suffolk pubs with a smuggling connection. It supposedly has a hidden cupboard under the eaves where contraband was stored.

2. Enter the marina via the roadway and be aware that the pathway in the second section becomes unclear. Just continue through the boats to the end and pick up the river wall again. Carry on past the top of Levington Creek and when shortly after you come back to the main river and reach a thick hedge, head away from the river towards the church on the hill.

3. If you can resist the obvious temptations of the 'Ship' when you reach the road, turn right and walk along the reasonably quiet lane for just over 1km. When you reach the road leading down to the Suffolk Yacht Harbour, turn right and, just after the start of a wood on your right, turn left across fields.

4. When this path eventually reaches some farm buildings, bear left between the barns to a stile and go over it. Cross a small paddock to your right to another stile, leading to the farm drive. At the end of the drive, turn right. This track turns to the left before passing in front of some brick cottages, and then runs downhill to the edge of a wood, then continues straight ahead, over an open field, uphill to a farm track.

5. Turn right and just before a gate, *** turn left into an avenue of small trees. On reaching a road, bear right and then, at the farm buildings, go left.

6. Just before you reach the next farm, turn right and follow the path for 150m before passing into a small area of wood to your left. Skirt the pond and turn right along a field edge. After 70m, turn left through a belt of trees.

7. As you emerge from the trees, take the path ahead just to the right of a cottage. At the field corner, continue straight ahead on a broad track. At the road, turn right and return to the start.

*** SHORTCUT: Turn right on the track just before the loompits and, after passing through a gate after about 700m, go into an avenue of small trees on your right.

WALK SIXTEEN

The Strand - Freston - Alton Water - Tattingstone - Belstead - Wherstead - The Strand

The Orwell, with Ipswich at its head and shelter from high banks on either side, has always been more important as a trading river than its near neighbours, the Deben and the Stour. Traces of Saxon quays found in Ipswich show for how long ships have plied this route and made it one of the major trading centres of northwest Europe.

In 1199 King John granted a charter giving the river to the people of Ipswich for all time. This ownership gradually extended downriver until eventually it reached almost all the way to Felixstowe and this means that the Orwell is one of the few British rivers not now owned by the crown.

Ownership brought the responsibility for dealing with the river's major problem - silt. As ships grew larger and larger, passage became more difficult. Dredging began in 1805 and has continued ever since, first by hand and, later, by mechanical dredger. The ship, Samuel Alexander, named after the main contributor to the subscription raised to build the first dredger, can be seen working on the river today as the battle to keep the river navigable continues.

In 1830, with the increase in trade due to the improvements made to the upper reaches of the Orwell, it was decided to build a wet dock in Ipswich. This was to allow ships to lie afloat at the Ipswich quays and larger vessels to use the port. When completed, it was the largest enclosed wet dock in Britain.

In the heyday of sail, all sorts of boats would have used the river: square riggers bringing timber from the Baltic and grain from Canada; steamers, running from Wherry Quay, ferrying passengers down to Harwich, or perhaps just on day excursions to Pin Mill or Felixstowe; topsail schooners and brigantines too. Ketch barges or 'boomies', spritsail barges or 'spritties': all would have graced the river at some time.

We are all familiar with the russet sailed barges on the river today. Now they are used for pleasure but they were once the workhorses of the river, used for all manner of everyday tasks. Coprolite and cement would be brought from the Deben: large vessels would be unloaded in Butterman's Bay and their goods taken as far afield as the Medway towns and Yarmouth, as well as up river to Ipswich. Large numbers were used to supply the capital with farm produce, as well as straw and feed for the enormous horse population. These barges would have the unsavoury task of returning laden with "London mixture", in other words horse muck, to spread on the fields.

Looking at the enormous container ships as they plough up and down the river today, I can only think how much more in keeping with the scale of the Orwell were the ships of yesteryear.

The Walk - 19km (11.75 miles)
Shorter Walk is 4km (2.5 miles)

At the beginning of May Freston woods are delightful: bluebells, archangel, campion and wild garlic provide a range of aromas.

Parking is best on the hard area on your left, as the road out of Ipswich climbs away from the Strand as you approach Freston. Tattingstone White Horse is a short detour from the walk if you require refreshment.

Sometimes, mainly due to winter ploughing, the path as you return to the fields close to the start is difficult to follow. It is probably best on these occasions to return via the road along the Strand.

START: Go down the hill and across the road. Opposite are two footpath signs: take the one on your left, crossing the stile to follow the right hand edge of the field. The OS map shows the footpath crossing the corner of the field but, especially when there are crops in the field, it is probably easier to follow the field edge.

2. At the oak tree, cross the stile on your right and take the left hand edge of the field, to a stile leading into woodland. Climb the hill to Freston church and, at the road, turn right and proceed until you are just past the lodge cottage, then take the track to the right. As you approach a house, bear left before rejoining the track and reaching a road.

3. Cross the road and turn right through a meadow. In the second field, swing right and follow the track all the way to Redgate Lane where you turn left. ***

4. As the road turns sharply right, turn left down a farm road and through open fields. As you pass through Valley Farm, turn left, then quickly right, to follow the right hand edge of the field. At the end of the field, the path enters woodland. Veer off to the right on the smaller path which follows the overhead wires. 70m after the path emerges into open fields, turn right to follow the track through Holbrook Park Woods and down to the road near Alton Water.

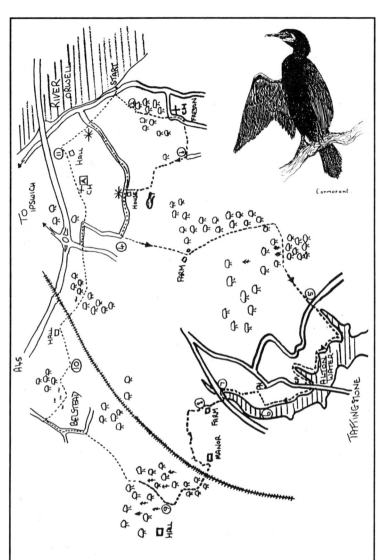

Cormorant

A. Until around 1900 Wherstead Church was topped by a large black ball serving as a navigation aid for boats coming up Downham Reach.

5. Cross the road and approach the reservoir. Take the right hand fork as the path splits; follow the edge of the reservoir to Tattingstone bridge. Cross the road and continue along the water's edge.

6. Just before the path enters the conservation area, cross a stile on your right and head uphill to pass cottages on your right. At a junction of paths, head to the left of the allotments ahead. After crossing a meadow, regain the reservoir path, turning right to reach the road.

7. Turn left, follow the road for 100m then cross over and head for Hubbards Hall. The path goes through a field to the right of the farm buildings, then through a gap in the hedge on the left and onto a track.

8. Turn right and, after 200m, left on a farm track. Follow this track to the railway, then turn right to cross the bridge and enter woodland. This track eventually meets a T-junction, as you approach Bentley Old Hall, where you turn right to enter woodland once more.

9. The track takes you through woods and fields towards Belstead Village. As you reach the road, turn left into the village. Look out for a footpath signposted on your right by a white bungalow. Follow the path, through scrub and bracken, to a field edge. Turn left and, at the corner of the wood, take the track ahead over a field.

10. Turn left and, as you pass Thorington Hall, turn right to cross the field and go under a railway bridge. The path passes through heath and woods to Wherstead. Go through the village and, where the road turns left, carry straight on, past the church and Wherstead Hall.

11. The path turns right just past the Hall, to cross fields and back to your start point. If the fields have been recently ploughed, or it is very wet, carry on down to the river and return via the Strand.***

*** SHORTCUT: As the path reaches the road at Redgate House, turn right and go down the quiet lane. At the bottom of the hill, at Redgate Farm, turn right over the field. If there is no sign of the path due to recent ploughing, carry on to the Strand and turn right.

WALK SEVENTEEN

Pin Mill - Woolverstone - Chelmondiston -
Clamp House - Pin Mill

Whilst researching this book it became apparent that the meaning and origin of many names have become lost in the mists of time. This has the disadvantage of one not knowing for certain why things are as they are, but the advantage that you can decide on whichever explanation suits you best.

This brings me to the Butt and Oyster at Pin Mill. There seems to be three stories as to how Suffolk's best known riverside pub got its name. Firstly, as depicted on the pub sign, the butt could have been the small barrel used to hold and transport the oysters. Secondly, it may be that in mediaeval times local archers could have practiced their skills at nearby butts or, thirdly, and this is my favourite as it came from a local source, a butt is a name for a flatfish (as in halibut) that made, with the oysters, the majority of the catch of the local fishermen.

Pin Mill itself poses problems. It could be very boringly from the old word for pond which was pynd so the pond which drove the mill was the pynd mill, or more intriguingly from the tale that a rich local landowner bestowed the income from the mill to his daughter as pin money. Most likely, however, is the story that the small stream running into the Orwell here was once the river Pindle and the hamlet was named after the mill on this river. The person who told me this one, however, may have been confusing Pindle with Grindle which is the old Suffolk word for a small stream.

As well as the Butt and Oyster, another building about which different stories are told is The Cat House next to the marina at Woolverstone. If you are very tall, or prepared to leap up and down in an athletic fashion, you should be able to see a white china cat in the window. It is said that a white paper cat was placed in the window either as a signal to smugglers that the coast was clear or, and here life does get confusing, that customs officers were in the vicinity. I suppose it is alright as long as the smugglers knew which was correct. However, the Reverend Richard Cobbold, writing in the mid-nineteenth century, said that it got its name when the gamekeeper lost his favourite cat in a rabbit trap. He had it stuffed and placed in the window where it was clearly visible to sailors as they travelled up and down the river and they named it The Cat House.

So there you are. Different places, different stories. As they say, "You pays your money and you takes your choice".

The Walk - 8km (5 miles)
Shorter Walk is 4.5km (2.75 miles)

This walk is one of the best known in Suffolk and is therefore best avoided on busy weekends, but is good at other times. Parking at the car park in Pin Mill and food and drink at the Butt and Oyster is my recommendation.

START: Walk down the road to the river and turn left to follow the track over the small stream. Just beyond the boatyard turn left away from the river, past Pin Mill Sailing Club. At the bridleway turn right and after 100m pass through the horse gate into open country.

2. You are now following the path upstream to Woolverstone Marina. Whenever the path forks, take the path nearer the river. When you reach the yacht club building pass in front of it then turn left immediately afterwards.

3. Just after the entrance to the marina buildings, turn left by a paling fence into the woodland, then take the narrow path off to your right a few metres before the "Private Keep Out" sign. Carry on through the woodland on the pathway, roughly following the line of the small stream.

4. At the road by the church, turn left then quickly right before crossing a stile on your left signposted to Chelmondiston. Two paths may be worn on the grass here and, if this is so, take the right hand one which leads to a stile on the far side of the parkland. Carry on across fields towards Chelmondiston. ***

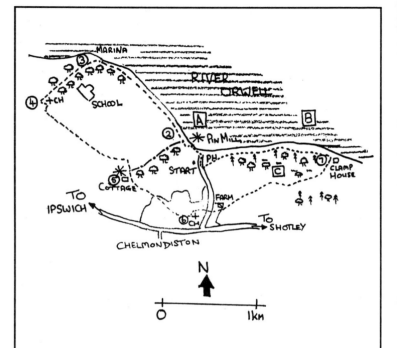

A. Looking at the hustle and bustle of the crowded river today, it is difficult to cast your mind back to the year 1016AD and imagine Cnut sailing upriver in his longship, or even just back to 1561AD when Queen Elizabeth sailed down the river to Shotley.

B. Butterman's Bay is named after the 'butter rigged' schooners which used to lay up here before proceeding with the tide up the river to Ipswich.

C. Cliff Plantation was extensively damaged in the great storm of October 1987. It was due to be replanted with native trees but, luckily, the government's stewardship scheme has allowed a plan to be put in place to restore a large part of it as grassland heath, a habitat of which Suffolk is short, so much having been destroyed by building and agriculture in recent years.

5. Shortly after you pass a white boarded cottage on your right, take a path rising off to your left. Follow this path, crossing a road, until you arrive at the church.

6. Turn left to take the road until you reach the Pin Mill road at a T-junction, cross and take the track opposite, passing through farm buildings and bearing left down to the river at Clamp House.

7. Just before you reach the house, turn left into the National Trust land between a pond and a black barn. It is better to keep to the upper path as you pass through Cliff Plantation to avoid high tide problems at the Butt and Oyster. The path eventually brings you out a few yards up the road from the car park, so turn right to find your car.

*** SHORTCUT: As the path swings away downhill to your right, take the bridleway to your left back towards Pin Mill. Where the main track bears left, carry on ahead downhill, turning right at the bottom to get back to Pin Mill.

Pin Mill.

WALK EIGHTEEN

Shotley Gate - Erwarton - Wade's Lane - Shotley Gate

I always thought the Bubonic Plague, or Black Death, left these shores many years ago and was surprised to find out that I was mistaken. The last outbreaks in this country were in Glasgow in around 1900 and on the Shotley Peninsula between 1906 and 1918.

The symptoms of the disease sound really horrible. The sufferer would fall into a fever, with a temperature rising to around 103 deg.F. The lymph glands would swell up, the skin become hot and dry and the tongue furred. Raging thirst, prostration and utter weakness would soon follow, with stupor or delirium accompanied by vomitting. The swollen glands, known as buboes (hence bubonic) occurred in the groin and armpit. Then haemorrhages would occur under the skin which sometimes produced black gangrenous patches (hence Black Death), which could lead to large ulcers. Normally the disease was fatal but sometimes the fever would abate and the buboes burst, disgorging foul smelling pus, and the patient eventually recovered.

The walk that follows seems to be a macabre tour of the places where the plague last occurred, but this was not intentional. The first outbreak was at Charity Farm Cottages in Wades Lane, Shotley, on December 9th, 1906. As I said, bubonic plague is a virulent and fast acting disease and the victim, a 53 year old woman, died three days later. Two more people caught the disease that month and one of them died.

Less than a month later, in the new year, another outbreak occurred at Brickhill Terrace Cottages, a quarter of a mile away from the previous site. Over the next few years, further cases were reported from Freston and at the naval barracks at Shotley Gate. There was then a gap of several years, to 1918, when there was an outbreak at Warren Lane, Erwarton, where two more women died.

Where did the virus come from? The main carrier of the plague virus is the flea of the black rat (Rattus Rattus). Like most fleas, while using its host for breeding purposes, it is only too happy to bite any warm blooded animal that passes its way, thereby transferring its deadly virus to humans. Local people believed the rats arrived with the barge loads of 'London mixture', the name given to horse muck which was brought back from the capital at that time. There is no evidence for this, as there was no plague in London then. While the outbreak was going on there was an understandable reluctance to eat locally caught rabbits and hares, in case they had caught the disease. A number of domestic animals, such as ferrets and cats, were certainly affected.

Turnstone.

The Walk - 13km (8 miles)
Shorter Walk is 11km (6.75 miles)

This walk features two rivers and a trek over the top of the Shotley Peninsula. Parking near the Bristol Arms in Shotley Gate, refreshment is available here or at the Old Boot Inn, halfway along the walk. From May to September the river bank between Orwell Cottages and Crane's Hill does become overgrown, but this section can easily be avoided, if necessary, by taking the shortcut via Shotley Church.

START: Turn right to go upstream. Walk to the end of the built up path, then follow the steps up the cliff to the road. Turn left and, at the end of the road, join the footpath.

2. Follow the path upriver as far as Erwarton Sluice, passing through the cottages and caravan park, as signposted along the way.

3. After crossing the small brick bridge at Erwarton Sluice, turn right to head inland towards the church. Keep on this track to pass round the right side of a small reservoir and along a delapidated avenue of sweet chestnuts to the road.

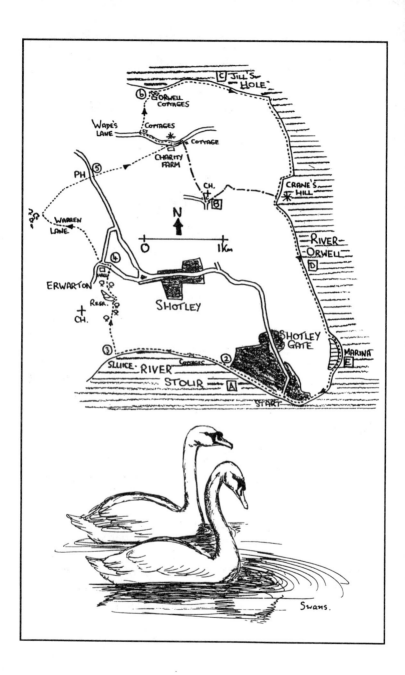

Swans.

A. You are now opposite Copperas Bay on the Essex side of the Stour. There was once a large industry collecting copperas which appears in the form of cylindrical lumps resembling pieces of wood. It comes out of the London clay and can be found along the sea shore and river banks of the area. Fleets of small fishing smacks made part of their living by dredging it up from the sea bed. The copperas, or iron sulphate extracted from it, was used for making ink, dyeing cloth and leather black, and for making the yellow wash used to colour many East Anglian cottages. Large amounts were also taken to a factory in Ipswich in order to make Sulphuric Acid.

B. At the crossroads near the church you have the strange sight of postboxes immediately opposite each other on this narrow road. You will have a frustrating time trying to post anything in the Victorian box, as it is sealed.

C. Jill's Hole, once an anchorage, was probably named after Richard Gylys, a local mariner, who died in 1530.

D. The mudflats here have been badly eroded by the wash from large boats and by rising sea levels. The Suffolk Wildlife Trust, in conjunction with Babergh District Council, has been active in an award winning scheme to provide a softer alternative to the usual concrete sea walls. First of all, a double row of stakes is driven into the mud and then the space in between is filled with brushwood which is then lashed into place. Already, after only two or three years, you can detect a real build up of mud and sand in this area.

E. The tip of the Shotley Peninsula is called Bloody Point. It was here in 885AD that a sea battle was fought in which Guthrum, the Danish King of East Anglia, was defeated by Alfred the Great. It is said that sixteen Danish ships were sunk and their crews killed.

4. Turn left, then second right opposite Erwarton Hall Gateway, along Warren Lane. When you come to a block of woodland on your left, take the footpath signposted over the field on your right. After crossing two fields, you emerge on the road at the Old Boot Inn.

5. Cross and take the footpath opposite, which becomes a track to Charity Farm on Wade's Lane. *** Turn left and, after 500m, right, down a track just after passing some cottages.

6. At the bottom of the hill you reach Orwell Cottages. Turn left to reach the river bank. When you are there, turn right for the 6km walk back along the river bank, *** first to the marina at Bloody Point, then on round the corner back to the car park.

*** SHORTCUT: Turn right and, after 100m, right again, just before a low cottage. Follow this track to Shotley Church, where you turn left and, at the T-junction at the bottom of the hill, right. Go through the gate ahead, into meadows. Keep the hedge on your left and carry on to the river bank. Here you turn right to rejoin the main path.

Long Tailed Duck

WALK NINETEEN

Lower Holbrook - Harkstead - Erwarton - Harkstead - Lower Holbrook

The Shotley Peninsula, so close to Ipswich yet still with a timeless, remote and tranquil landscape, was designated an Area of Outstanding Natural Beauty in 1969. Since then, firstly, the Shotley Peninsula Countryside Project and, now, the Suffolk Coast and Heaths Project, run by the local councils, have worked to maintain and enhance the unique character of the area.

The vulnerable lowland landscape, created as a result of man and nature working together over the centuries, has changed considerably over recent years. Housing development, changes in agricultural practice, Dutch elm disease and the storm of October 1987 have all contributed to landscape decline and loss of wildlife. Just one example is that of primroses; once abundant, they have now been picked or sprayed to the edge of extinction.

The Shotley Peninsula Project Officer tries to work to improve and conserve what is good in the area. Having little statutory power, he must reconcile the ideas of conservation and recreation organisations, local industry and the people that live and work on the peninsula. In addition, there are the views of the ever growing number of visitors that are drawn to and enjoy the area.

As you walk around the region it may not be immediately obvious what influence the project is having, but a little investigation will show all sorts of different schemes going on. For instance, ten leaflets have been published describing a selection of walks. These had to be waymarked and maintained, all of which meant providing stiles, gates, bridges and steps to assist access. In places, such as along the bank of the stream in Holbrook, levelling and strengthening work was undertaken. A circular cycling route has been developed and a guide published. The saltmarsh, being extremely fragile, has to be protected so vehicles have had to be controlled along The Strand. Where the marsh is being eroded along the Orwell, near Shotley, by industrial pressure and rising sea levels, groynes have been built to protect what is left. The tiny patch of remnant grassland heath at

Chelmondiston must be mowed and raked yearly, and areas of wood-land at Woolverstone, Wherstead and Brantham Decoy pond all managed in traditional fashion. Long stretches of hedgerow and hundreds of individual trees have also been planted. In some places, particularly near the rivers, there are still some fields of 'unimproved' grassland. Containing plants that don't exist in any other habitat, it is important they are kept as they are, for once 'improved' by spraying, feeding or reseeding, it is nearly impossible to restore them to their former glory. Farmers are, therefore, encouraged, with the help of grants, to leave them as they are.

So, as you enjoy the area, take notice and see how much has been done to enhance your pleasure. Perhaps you will be able to put something back by shopping in the village shops or taking refreshment in one of the many public houses.

The Walk - 14.5km (9 miles)
Shorter Walk is 8km (5 miles)

A small car park in Lower Holbrook is the starting point for this walk. The only hazard you are likely to encounter is if you keep to the beach rather than the river bank for too long between Harkstead and Erwarton: you eventually find it is too muddy to make your way back to the river bank and have to retrace your steps. The Baker's Arms at Harkstead provides excellent home cooked meals.

START: Go down the track to the river and, when you get there, turn left and follow the beach for around 2.5km, then the river bank *** for about 4km.

2. When you reach Erwarton Sluice, it is time to go inland. This is marked by a footpath sign, which is pointing to your left, just past Erwarton church, which you can see on the hill about 750m inland. Take the track passing to the right, round the small reservoir, through the sweet chestnut avenue, to the road.

3. Turn left, and then right along Warren Lane, as you come to

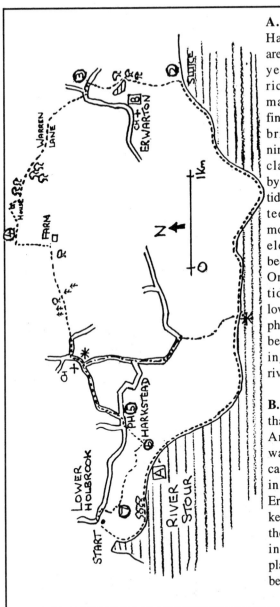

A. The Harkstead Cliff area has, over the years, proved rich in mammalian bone finds. A seam of brickearth running through the clay is exposed by the winds and tides. Bones and teeth of mammoth, bison and elephant have been found here. Once, when the tide was really low, a pair of elephant tusks could be seen protruding through the river mud.

B. Legend has it that the heart of Anne Boleyn was placed in a casket and buried in the church at Erwarton. A casket was found in the chancel wall in 1837 and placed in a vault below the organ.

Erwarton Hall gateway. After 1.5km you reach a house. Very inconveniently, the path passes round this house to the right, before turning left to rejoin the track.

4. Follow the track for 500m until you reach a track coming in from your left. Take this and, at the T-junction, turn right. At the road, go straight ahead and, at the junction, turn left to take the road past the church. *** (Do not turn left here).

5. At the main road turn right and, just past the Baker's Arms, left. After 30m, turn right on the footpath signposted to the River Stour.

6. On reaching the road at Shore Cottage, turn right, and, after 150m, left across the field. After another 200m, take the footpath to your right, signposted to Holbrook Creek.

7. At the end of a long hedge on your right, you come to a crossroads of paths. Follow the hedge round the edge of the field to the road. Turn left and, after 150m, left into the car park.

*** SHORTCUT: The riverbank path meets a path coming in by a hedge across a field on your left. Follow the hedge inland to a track, turn left and, at the road, left again. After about 500m, take the minor road on your right to Harkstead church where you rejoin the main walk, turning left.

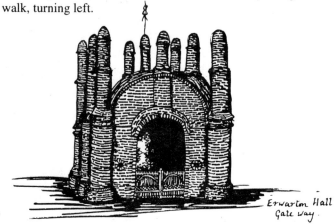

Erwarton Hall Gateway.

WALK TWENTY

Alton Water - Holbrook - Stutton - Alton Water

How marvellous it feels to walk along the banks of the Stour and hear what, to me, is the definitive sound of the Suffolk estuaries. The shrill penetrating "kleep kleep" of a small group of oystercatchers as they rise from the mudflats and fly past. It never fails to send a chill down my spine and engenders a feeling of being glad to be alive and able to enjoy this beautiful area.

The river Stour is a really wonderful place for watching ducks, geese and waders. To be considered important, an area must contain at least 1% of the national or international total for any particular species. The Stour is internationally important for species such as Brent goose, shelduck, grey plover, redshank and, in particular, black tailed godwit, which, with around 700 birds, is the second largest population in Britain. It is also nationally important for mute swans, wigeon, ringed plover and dunlin. Totals are large indeed. Over 12,000 dunlin, 1,000 Brent geese, 1,700 wigeon and 1,300 mallard give some idea of the large numbers which gather each winter. If you are on the lookout for the less common species, you may be lucky and spot the odd sanderling or red breasted merganser.

The first section of river you come to on this walk is probably also the best area on the northern bank. Having come along the stream from Holbrook, you may have been lucky enough to catch the unmistakable blue and orange flash of a kingfisher, darting away from one of the small bridges along the brook. You then come to the area around Holbrook Creek and the lagoons infront of Holbrook School. Here you will find lots of waders with knot, grey plover, dunlin and turnstone often being present. Ducks and geese such as Brent geese, shelduck, wigeon and pintail are often there in quantity. Birds find the stumps and derelict banks of the old lagoons very attractive, because they can rest undisturbed, and you may see the occasional grebe actually on a lagoon.

The next good section is below the cliff, as you approach the mill at Stutton. As the cliff is heavily wooded here, and access to the beach limited, the birds obviously feel well protected. Large numbers of

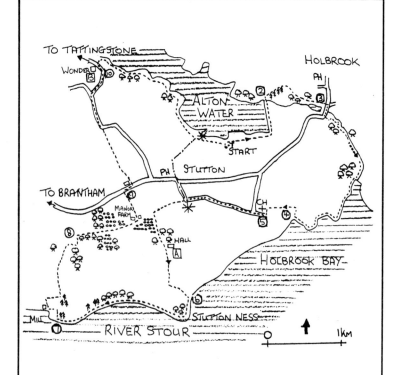

A. In 1890, the owners of Crepping Hall thought that a viable seam of coal ran under the Stour from Stutton to Harwich. They sank a shaft, reaching a depth of 1,500ft, before giving up the search. I am glad they did: the idea of the Shotley peninsula as the Barnsley of East Anglia is too awful to think about.

B. In 1750, Edward White, the owner of Tattingstone Hall, wanted to improve the view across the valley outside his house. To kill two birds with one stone, he built Tattingstone Wonder, a folly consisting of cottages faced with a false church front and tower.

Brent geese can be spotted here. Sometimes mute swans wander across from their Mistley home. It is thought that the swans were originally attracted by the masses of waste from the maltings. Now these are no longer operating, the population is probably maintained here by the large number of people who like to stop and feed them along the Promenade at Mistley.

King Fisher.

The Walk - 18km (11.25 miles)
Shorter Walk is 8.5km (5.25 miles)

The area between Stutton Ness and Stutton Mill, with its fine wooded cliff, is one of my favourite river walks. There is the bonus of a section along the edge of Alton Water, plus the delights of the stream running down to the river at Holbrook Creek. Parking is at the Alton Water car park where, in the summer, the cafe is open for refreshment. For those taking the short walk, a detour to The King's Head in Stutton is recommended.

START: Walk towards the lake, following the road round to the right as far as the dam. Cross the dam and follow the chain link fence to the right hand corner of the grassed area.

2. Take the permissive path away from the reservoir. Where the main path turns away uphill, continue ahead

Redshank.

101

to follow the fence over a brook on your right. Cross a stile and continue to the road.

3. Turn right towards the mill and, at the corner, take the footpath off to the left. This path follows the stream to Holbrook Creek. When you arrive there, turn right, and go on to the hideously ugly boathouse. Turn left after this to follow the river wall for 1km.

4. Go down the steps to your right and follow the path along the right hand edge of the field. At the end, turn left to follow the green lane. At the house, continue ahead towards the church.

5. When you reach the road, continue straight on into Stutton village until you reach a sharp right hand corner. *** Continue ahead here, first on a track and then on a path. When you reach a juntion of three roads, turn left, following the road, and then the track, to the river.

6. At the river, turn right and enjoy the fine walk and views along the bank.

7. Just before you reach Stutton Mill, go right on the permissive path, then left, after passing through a hedge, to skirt the buildings and gardens, before turning right on reaching the lane.

8. After about 1km, you pass a lodge and woods on your right. Turn right and continue until you have just passed Manor Farm on your left. Turn left on a lane between cottages and carry on as far as the main road.

9. Turn right and, after passing the community centre and cottages, left to follow the footpath across a field. At the far side of the field, go straight ahead on the track. Where this joins the road, turn left and, when Tattingstone is signposted on your right, take this road as far as Tattingstone Wonder.

10. A stile on your right takes you back into the reservoir area. After crossing the stile, take one of the paths by the lake back towards the

car park, bearing in mind that when water levels are high the paths nearest the lake edge flood. ****

*** SHORTCUT: As you come to the right-angle bend in Stutton, follow the road round to the right until you reach the main road. Cross and go up the lane opposite. After 300m, go through a gap in the hedge on your right, and take the path following the telephone wires back towards the reservoir. When you get back there, turn right.

Holbrook
School.

WALK TWENTY-ONE

Cattawade - Brantham - Bentley - East End - Cattawade

Until the 1940s, the multitude of wintering wildfowl of the Suffolk river estuaries provided a valuable resource for the local population. Food for the table and money in the pocket after selling their catch in the markets of London; both were useful.

The three main ways of killing birds were by wildfowling, puntgunning and the use of decoy ponds. Today, wildfowling is enjoyed by about 150,000 people around Britain, accounting for over 1,000,000 birds annually - mainly mallard, wigeon, teal and a variety of geese. Taking wigeon as an example of a bird which is shot mainly in coastal regions, rather than inland, some estimate that up to 50% of the wintering population of 224,000 is killed each year.

Puntgunning still occurs in East Anglia and nine puntgunners are registered along the coast, mainly based on the Stour around Manningtree. This barbaric means of killing involves using a large bore shotgun, like an old fashioned blunderbuss, fixed in the bows of the boat. Lying low in the punt, and preferably with the moon ahead of the gunner to keep him in the dark, he would paddle gently towards the flocks of ducks in the hope of getting as close as possible to make the maximum possible kill, before blasting away. In the 1930s, a haul of 80 birds with one shot was recorded, though 6-10 fowl was a more normal bag. Any severely injured birds would be finished off with a 12 bore shotgun.

Just looking quickly at a map of the area, I can find decoy ponds at Brantham, Falkenham, Nacton, Purdis Heath, Waldringfield and Shottisham. Clearly these ponds were important to the local economy. The simplest way of trapping birds is to erect lines of nets across the fens and marshes and, when it gets dark, the wildfowl fly into them. It is obviously more efficient if you are able to lure the birds to one spot to kill them and, with this in mind, the idea of decoy ponds was formulated.

Firstly, a pond was dug with several side channels leading out from it. These were covered with netting, forming gradually narrowing pipes or tunnels. A small dog was then employed to run the length of the tunnel, away from the pond, before disappearing behind a screen. This fascinated the naturally inquisitive ducks and, slowly, drew them into the tunnels where they were easily trapped. The number of birds caught in this fashion was truly amazing. At the Nacton decoy, where a good record was kept by the owner, Colonel Tomline, in 18 years almost 18,000 birds were taken. The record year accounted for 3,000 birds. This fits in well with the returns from the Iken decoy where, in a good season, the decoyman estimated that he took 3,000 fowl and claimed a record bag of 501 duck in one day.

The Walk - 15km (9.5 miles)
Shorter Walk 1 is 9km (5.5 miles)
Shorter Walk 2 is 12.5km (9.75 miles)

After parking at the top of Cattawade Street, you will find that this walk has a rather inauspicious start through the housing estate. That is soon compensated for by good river, woodland and meadow walking. A short detour by the railway bridge will bring you to refreshment at the Brantham Bull. Good footwear is essential as there are sometimes sloshy areas in the woods at Dodnash and Bentley.

START: Park at the top of Cattawade Street, near the old school (now a photographic studio) and go up the road opposite into the housing estate. At the top of the hill, turn right into Merrion Close and right again after the playground.

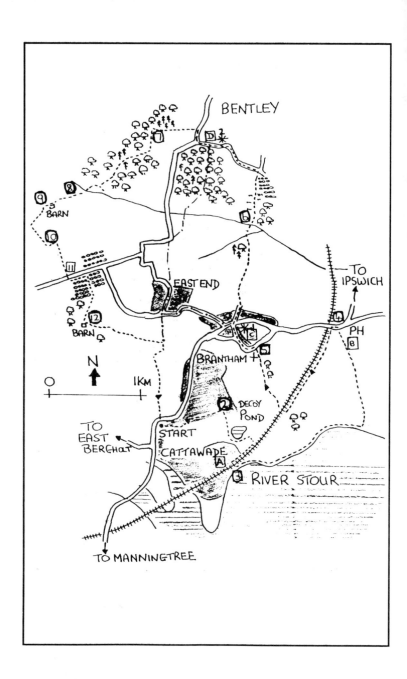

BENTLEY

BARN

EAST END

BARN

TO IPSWICH

PH

BRANTHAM

DECOY POND

N

0   1KM

TO EAST BERGHOLT

START

CATTAWADE

RIVER STOUR

TO MANNINGTREE

A. The complex of factories at Brantham is based on what was, 100 years ago, the British Xylonite Company Works and is still known as that by some local people. Xylonite (from the Greek, xylon, meaning wood) was a synthetic replacement for ivory and tortoiseshell. The factory made imitation ivory combs and piano keyboards, plastic shirt fronts, collars and cuffs that did not need laundering, table tennis balls and dice. Several attempts have been made to plant trees to shield this ugly site from the river but the high salt content of the land has made this impractical.

B. Crinkle crankle walls, also known as ribbon or serpentine walls, are found scattered throughout southeastern Britain but the great majority are found in Norfolk and Suffolk, particularly around Yarmouth and Gorleston. Mainly late Georgian, brick built and with a distinct wavy shape, it is possible they are another example of the Dutch influence in East Anglian building, as both ports mentioned had strong trading links with Holland where these walls are also found. Extremely pleasing to look at, they have the practical advantage of providing warm alcoves for fruit to ripen in the gardens.

Crinkle Crankle Wall.

C. Brantham takes its name from the Saxon for burnt village. The Danes raided along the Stour in 991 AD and burnt the settlement to the ground.

D. The roadside at Dodnash Woods is a good site to see the rare Wild Service Tree, with its maple-like leaves and small brown berries which are just about sweet enough to eat. The leaves of a related tree were used to sweeten beer: the Latin for beer is cerevisia, which we later corrupted to service.

2. Go downhill, passing the decoy pond on your left and then join another path, turning left, then right, to pass round the end of the factories to the railway line. Turn right to go behind the factories until you reach a stile to take you over the railway.

3. Cross and join the river bank walk for 1.5km. When leaving the river, ignore the first path inland, continue past the dead trees on the mudflats and past a field on your left. Go inland on the path immediately opposite the maltings at Mistley.

4. At the main road, turn left and, after 150m, left again, just before the railway bridge. Follow the railway line and, after passing one bridge, cross at the second. After crossing the bridge, turn right to go through an avenue of poplars to the church.

5. At the road, turn left and follow this road to the main one. 1 *** Cross and go down Gravelpit Lane. As the lane bears to the right, carry on down a path, through an archway of trees, to an old farm gate and stile on the left leading through to a meadow. Follow the sloping right hand side of the meadow to a metal gate. Climb the gate and walk diagonally to the right to a concrete bridge over a brook.

6. The waymarked path continues until you reach the drive of Dodnash Priory Farm. Take the drive down to the crossroads and turn left to follow the minor road for 1km, passing Dodnash Woods on your left. 2 *** Turn right at the junction and, after 150m, left on the footpath.

7. At the end of the field, at a crossroads of paths, turn left and, on reaching the woodyard, turn right to pass to the left of the buildings. At a fork in the track, keep to the left. After a while, the track narrows to a path; descend the hill and, at the bottom, turn right, keeping the reed bed on your left. After about 250m, a short path on your left takes you to a low plank over the stream.

8. Find a way up the bank and through the trees to a stile into the meadow. Cross, bearing slightly to the right to a bridge over the

river.

9. Turn right to pass round the edge of the field to a stile into a meadow. At the far corner, soon after passing a barn on your left, cross a stile to your left. After 250m, take the signposted path to your left, leaving the meadow at the far corner. Keep the hedge to your right as you go through the field.

10. Turn left at the poplars to pass round the field to the road.

11. Cross and enter the orchard at the corner. The path is marked by waymarks as you cross the orchard but they may be hidden by trees. If this is the case, follow the line of the road until just before the third shelter belt, and then cross: you should reach a stile on the far side. Go over and, after keeping the field edge on your right, go through a small gate.

12. Turn left at the crossroads of paths, immediately passing through a gap in the left hand hedge. As you reach a gravel track, keep following the line of the hedge until you reach a T-junction. 1 & 2 ***. Turn right and follow this meandering track down to the A137. Cross and return to the start.

*** SHORTCUTS:

1. As the road emerges on the A137 opposite Gravelpit Lane, turn left and, after 100m, right into Slough Lane. After 800m, as you come to a road on your right, take the track opposite. The main path joins yours from the right after 300m.

2. Shortly after the start of Dodnash Woods, on your left, take the signposted path through the woods. At the end of the wood, bear right through a wet meadow. Cross a wooden bridge and go straight ahead up a hill over a field. When the path emerges on the road, take the footpath on the left, across farmland to a children's playground. Follow the road ahead to the main road, cross and after 300m, the main path joins from the right.

TWO LINEAR WALKS

There are two walks which I was unable to fit into a convenient circular format but consider well worth doing as straightforward there and back walks.

WALK TWENTY-TWO

Firstly, we have the old sailor's path from Aldeburgh to Snape. This path was used when there was a delay, either with the tide or with the time needed to load a vessel, and the sailors would return home using this path. If you park in the small car park opposite the golf course in Aldeburgh, the walk is 6.5km (4 miles) each way through very attractive woods, meadows, heath and river bank to Snape where refreshment is to be had at the pub or cafe.

Snape Maltings.

Take the track away from the car park and, where the path forks at the end of the houses, take the right hank fork to follow this path for 5km towards Snape. 10m before you reach a road, turn left through high gorse bushes. At a crossroads of paths, turn left and, after 25m, right. This path leads to the river bank where you turn right to go along the bank to Snape.

WALK TWENTY-THREE

The second walk is a beach walk from Southwold to Covehithe and back. After parking near the pier in Southwold, this walk of 5km (3 miles) each way is a good opportunity to study the rampant erosion on this part of the coast, as well as enjoying a spot of birdwatching on Easton and Covehithe Broads. Like the better known Benacre Broad a little further up the coast, they were both formed when the passage to the sea of these small rivers was blocked by a shingle bank.

BIBLIOGRAPHY

SUFFOLK COAST by N Scarfe. Published by The Alistair Press.

DISCOVERING THE SUFFOLK COAST by T Palmer. Published by Heritage House.

BUTTERFLIES OF SUFFOLK by H Mendel & S H Piotrowski. Published by Suffolk Naturalist's Society.

BELOVED COAST & SUFFOLK SANDLINGS by R A Whitehead. Published by Terence Dalton.

SUTTON HOO: EXCAVATION OF A ROYAL SHIP BURIAL by C Green. Published by Merlin Press.

SUFFOLK SANDLINGS by R Simper. Published by East Anglian Magazines.

SMUGGLERS OF THE SUFFOLK COAST by L P Thompson. Published by Brett Valley Publications.

SUFFOLK COAST by R Edwards. Published by Terence Dalton.

EAST ANGLIAN SHORES by D Fairhall. Published by Nautical.

SAVED FROM THE SEA by R Malster. Published by Terence Dalton.

RIVER STOUR by R Edwards. Published by Terence Dalton.

RIVER DEBEN and RIVER ORWELL. Both written by R Simper and published by Creekside Publications.

SUFFOLK ESTUARIES by Beardall, Dryden & Holzer. Published by Suffolk Wildlife Trust.

SUFFOLK ESTUARY by W G Arnott. Published by N Adlard & Co.

SUFFOLK WE LIVE IN by P Fincham. Published by Geo Nobbs.

PORTRAIT OF SUFFOLK by A Jobson. Published by Hale.

SMUGGLING IN EAST ANGLIA by S Jarvis. Published by Countryside Books.

FORGOTTEN RAILWAYS OF EAST ANGLIA by R S Joby. Published by David & Charles.

SHOTLEY PENINSULA and THE HEAVY HORSE by E Hart. Published by Shire Publications Ltd.

EYE ON THE HURRICANE by B Oxley & K Reynolds. Published by Froglets Publications.

BRANCH LINE TO SOUTHWOLD by V Mitchell & K Smith. Published by Middleton Press.